THE CAREER RESOURCE LIBRARY

Careers
in the

MOVIES

Marlys H. Johnson

The Rosen Publishing Group, Inc.
NEW YORK

Published in 2001 by The Rosen Publishing Group, Inc.
29 East 21st Street, New York, NY 10010

Library of Congress Cataloging-in-Publication Data

Johnson, Marlys H.
    Careers in the movies / by Marlys H. Johnson — 1st ed.
        p.   cm.
Includes index.
    ISBN 0-8239-3186-2 (lib. bdg.)
    1. Motion pictures—Vocational guidance—Juvenile litera-
ture. I. Title. II. Careers (Rosen Publishing Group)
    PN1995.9 .P75 J54   2000
    791.43'02'93—dc21   00-010220

Manufactured in the United States of America

About the Author

Marlys H. Johnson, M.Ed., is a professional writer who has written over fifty articles on business and health topics. She is also the author of two books, one on chemical dependency and one on exercise addiction.

Acknowledgments

Thank you to Beth Pike, Ed Richardson, and Steve Weinberg, and special thanks to Stephen Gardner for his support and encouragement.

Contents

Introduction

Did you every think about a career in the movies? Most young people dream of a career as a movie star. It certainly looks like a glamorous career when you see television shows about celebrities or magazines articles about their lifestyles. But there are many other careers in the movies. A movie production is a collaboration of hundreds of people doing many different kinds of jobs, from running errands to managing budgets to building sets. Did you know that you could have a job in the movies as a clapper loader or a best boy? How about working as a grip or a gaffer? These are actual jobs in the movies for people who do things like assist the director of photography or help set up the lights.

The movie business is not all glamour and glitz. Most of the people who work in the movies are not famous and work at jobs that are "behind the scenes." Most of the jobs in the movies involve hard work, long hours, and rigid deadlines. Everything has to be done on a schedule because equipment may have been rented or a location may be available for only a certain amount of time.

Who works on a movie will depend on the kind of movie production it is, whether it is an action-adventure

Careers in the Movies

film like *Mission: Impossible,* a modern horror movie like *Scream,* or a romantic comedy like *My Best Friend's Wedding.* Many stunt artists were needed for the incredible stunts and special effects in *Mission: Impossible.* It took many film extras for the crowd scenes in *My Best Friend's Wedding.*

The people who work on a movie production generally work in discrete departments or on crews. The departments are headed by the key people who are responsible for a particular type of creative work, like the director of photography, the art director, and the film editor. They work closely with the director of the movie, under his or her supervision, in fact. Most careers in the movie business mean you will belong to a union or guild. These organizations help negotiate working conditions and basic pay rates for their members. Most careers in the movies are not high-paying jobs. Unless you work as a department head, like an art director or costume designer, you will not make a huge salary.

There are more jobs available in movies today than in previous years. As the cable market has expanded, so has the demand for original movie productions. Made-for-TV movies are as popular as ever. There has also been a considerable increase in movie production in the direct-to-video market. You can also work in movie production for a corporation, producing training videos, or on independent films.

If you want to work in the movies today, you will have to know how to use computers. Computers are changing the way movies are produced and what kinds of jobs are available in the industry. No matter what your interest— math, science, writing, photography, business, theater, or acting—there is a career for you in the movies.

The History of Movie Production

1

The film industry today is a big-budget business that uses cutting-edge technology and sophisticated filmmaking techniques to bring a scriptwriter's story to life. The possibilities of what a film director can do are limited only by the latest production techniques. Even the modern movie theater is a techno-adventure. Stadium seating gives you a perfect view of the screen regardless of where you sit. Stereo surround sound hits you from every corner of the room. Even the armrests have been modernized for your convenience with popcorn and soda holders, all to make movie-going an enjoyable experience.

But it hasn't always been that way. Like most modern technologies, the motion picture industry has advanced over time as new filmmaking techniques and equipment have been developed. Most of the special effects, camera techniques, and lighting advances that you see in the movies today have been created because the director of the movie called for them or a scriptwriter wrote them into the screenplay. All this because of the increasing expectations of the movie-going audience.

Black Maria was Thomas Edison's first film studio.

The Motion Picture Camera

"Motion picture" means just that—a picture that is in motion. In 1877 in California, Eadweard Muybridge captured the motion of a horse at a full gallop for the first time. He set up twenty-four cameras alongside a racetrack with threads attached to the shutters of each camera. The threads were stretched across the track. As the horse went galloping past the cameras, it broke the threads and triggered the shutters. Each camera in succession took a picture of the horse as it galloped past. When the plates from each camera were developed and printed, Muybridge had a series of photographs showing the horse in what looked like continuous motion. Muybridge used a lantern to shine light through the pictures to project them onto a screen. As he changed quickly from photo to photo, it looked like the horse was in motion, a new concept for the time. But setting up a series of cameras to take pictures of a subject in motion was not practical. There had to be another way of showing what the series of photographs did: that motion could be captured on film.

Thomas Edison, the American inventor, heard Muybridge speak and began working on a new camera. Called a kinetograph, it took a series of pictures of moving objects. Edison also went on to make the first colorized film by coloring each frame of the film by hand. In England in the late 1800s, William Friese-Green also developed a motion picture camera. In America, George Eastman's company, working with a discovery of Rev. Hannibal Williston Goodwin, combined fusel oil and amyl acetate (banana oil) with celluloid and made a film that was strong, transparent, and flexible.

In France in the 1890s, the Lumiere brothers invented the "claw" mechanism. This device made it possible to advance film quickly. A series of hooks caught the film by the perforations, or holes, along its sides and pulled the next frame of the film into place. Take a special camera, a roll of film that allows you to take one picture after another, and a mechanism that pulls that film through the camera quickly, and you have a motion picture camera. The Latham family developed the "Latham loop." They added an extra sprocket to the wheel on the supply reel, which created a loop as the celluloid was pulled by the wheel to change frames. Edison combined the Latham loop with a gearshift mechanism and manufactured a projector called the Vitascope. With these advances came the ability to show the movie on a film projector.

There is a lot more to making a movie than having the right kind of camera. It takes a special setting that allows you to control the sound and lighting around you. It takes special kinds of lamps to illuminate indoor scenes, and special sound equipment that can record the dialogue of the actors without interference. To provide for these unique requirements, the sound stage was created.

In New Jersey in 1893, Thomas Edison's company built the first film studio. It was called the Kinetographic Theater, or Black Maria, because it was painted black inside and out. The studio had a revolving base that allowed it to move and follow the sun as it crossed the sky, allowing the action to be photographed all day. The first movie films required intense light to record an image because the camera lens is not as sensitive as the naked eye.

Advances in Sound and Color

The motion pictures of the early 1900s were far different from what you see at the movies today. The first motion pictures were only a few minutes in length, had no sound, and were called silent pictures. They were not completely silent, however. Sound was provided by a piano player in the movie theater who played along with the picture. Eventually a piano that played by itself, called a player piano, provided the sound.

The first motion pictures were in black and white. Color film had not been invented yet. The use of black-and-white film led to some sophisticated film-shooting techniques. The costumes, props, and set were used to enhance the look of the black-and-white film, with lighting effects used to create the mood.

In 1906, Lee de Forest invented the audion tube. Using electronic valves, as vacuum tubes were first called, de Forest amplified sounds picked up by a microphone. Sound was added to motion pictures by Edison in 1915 when he developed a phonograph disc that played in synchronization with the film. Sound was used in a picture called *Dream Street* by D.W. Griffith. Warner Brothers used a Vitaphone sound system in some of their films. In 1926, the movie *Don Juan* used the Vitaphone program successfully. It included a musical score, sound effects of swords clashing and horse's hooves galloping, and some short-subject pictures with speech and singing. But sound did not catch on in popularity with the movie audience at first. It took Al Jolson's singing in *The Jazz Singer* in 1927 to make sound in movies a popular demand. From then on, audiences wanted to see talking pictures, or "talkies."

The attempt to produce movies in color was first tried in 1906 in England by G. A. Smith, who used color filters to create a colored picture. In 1931, color film was invented by Herbert Kalmus. In the 1930s, with the addition of sound and color, movies started to look like what you see in the theaters today. Directors and movie studios continued to make movies in black and white, but by the 1950s these films declined in popularity. Today a movie is filmed in black and white only to create a certain mood or effect, such as the critically acclaimed *Schindler's List*, made in 1993 by director Steven Spielberg.

Advances in Special Effects

The first movie with special effects was made in 1902 by George Méliès and was called *A Trip to the Moon*. In 1933, the original movie version of *King Kong* required special effects that would make it appear that a giant gorilla was terrorizing New York. It would have been very difficult to make such a creature and then to control its motions and film it. The film was made possible after trick photography was introduced in 1900 by George Méliès in Paris. These early special effects were called "opticals."

In the early 1990s, a script called for creatures that roamed the earth millions of years ago; dinosaurs that many people had seen in books or archaeologists had re-created in museums. The director and special effects coordinator had a challenging task. How could they make these creatures using the existing technology, stop-motion film techniques, and models that had to be hand built in the special effects lab? It would take months to make all the models necessary and even more time to set up the scenes and advance the action from frame to frame. Thanks to computer animation, the realistic scenes you see in *Jurassic Park* were made digitally. Mark Dippe, working with Industrial Light and Magic, digitally created what looked like live, fully functioning dinosaurs, and showed them to Steven Spielberg, who directed the hugely successful *Jurassic Park*.

The Movie Theater

To show the pictures made at the Kinetographic Theater, Edison invented the kinetoscope. Audiences had to peer into the kinetoscope one person at a time to see the picture. The kinetoscope did not make it possible for a large group of people to watch the motion picture at the same time.

Two developments that contributed to the advancement of film-projection techniques were made around 1895. Robert Paul, working in England, and Woodville Latham, working in America, came up with techniques to project clear images onto a screen for the first time. From

The dinosaurs of *Jurassic Park* were created using digital technology.

then on, moving pictures were projected on to a screen and shown to audiences as a group. The Lumiere brothers of France also made a projector that would show a movie to several people at one time. In 1895, the first theater audience watched a movie made by the Lumiere brothers in the basement of a café in Paris. This was what many historians consider the first public showing of a movie. It was a newsreel the Lumiere brothers had made of their factory employees during lunch break. In 1896, in New York City, motion pictures were shown publicly for the first time in the United States.

The first organized movie screenings were seen in nickelodeons. People sat on benches or chairs to watch the movie. The movies were short, filmed in black and white, and silent. A piano player provided the only sound. The development of wide-screen projection techniques completed the process. Abel Gance first used wide-screen techniques in France in 1927. The techniques were used again in Hollywood in the 1950s. In the 1970s, the wide-screen technique was expanded in Canada through the Canadian IMAX system. Today wide theater screens, stereo surround sound, and stadium seating at multitheater cineplexes have made going to the movies a high-tech experience.

The Filming Process

If you have ever played around with a camcorder and shot some video, you have probably discovered that filming something is not as easy as it looks. When you look at the video later, you may discover that it looks a lot different from how you thought it would. You may have framed the subjects, the actors in your movie, incorrectly, with half the people in the camera's view and the others outside of it. The lighting may be bad. People may squint as they look directly into the sun. The video may appear washed-out with too much bright light or very dark from underexposure. The people in your movie may seem awkward and posed for the camera. The sound may be bad as you discover that you had the microphone too far away and you can't understand what people are saying. As is typical of most home movies, there are long gaps in the action and the video seems to drag on forever with not much of anything going on.

Making a movie is a carefully planned process designed to go as quickly and as efficiently as possible. The filming, or shooting, of the movie is usually done one scene at a time until the entire movie is completed. The movie script indicates the setting of the scenes, such as an apartment or an exotic location like a Caribbean beach. The script also indicates if a scene is an indoor, or interior, scene or an outdoor, or exterior, scene. From the movie script, the director and the direc-tor of photography determine how to film the movie, what locations to use, and what kinds of sets will be needed. Once a set is built, they determine the angles for filming and where to place the camera.

The scenes of a movie are not shot in order, that is, the filming does not follow the movie script from the beginning of the story to the end. The scenes are shot according to location or setting. If one scene in the beginning of the movie takes place on the Manhattan Bridge and the last scene of the movie takes place on the Manhattan Bridge, those two scenes will be shot one after the other. The movie is filmed in this way to save time and money.

Setting up a scene takes a lot of planning and hard work. The set must be built, and everything that goes in it must be put in place. For example, if the scene is an interior scene in a living room, all the furniture and anything that is used to decorate the set—pictures on the walls, lamps, plants, rugs, books in a bookcase—must be put in place for the scene according to the set design. The lighting for the scene has to be put up and focused. The microphones and sound recording equipment must be placed to record the dialogue of the actors. Because of all the work involved in preparing a set or location for filming, it is most efficient to film the scenes that use the same set or location together. Later, in the editing process, the scenes are put into the proper order by the film editor.

The Modern Big-Budget Picture

Modern movies have multimillion dollar budgets, and their producers have even bigger expectations about how well they will do at the box office. Because production costs have grown tremendously in recent years, the modern movie executive at a movie studio must look carefully at the potential cost of a movie when looking at a new script. Movie studios used to make one big-budget epic film a year. Today this is not possible, because even modest films require tens of millions of dollars to produce. Because of the huge costs of production, producers are expected to keep films under budget and on schedule. Costs have increased because of a combination of changes in the movie industry.

The salaries of movie stars have gone up tremendously in recent years. For example, a star like Leonardo

DiCaprio could expect to make about $1 to $2 million a picture in the early 1990s. Currently he can earn $10 to $12 million a picture and get a percentage of the profits at the box office. Production costs have also increased. Special effects, location costs, marketing and publicity, and crew costs have all increased, making movie production a high-cost business.

How a Movie Is Made

2

Do you ever stay until the end of the movie when the credits roll? The credits, or the listing of people who worked on the movie, include job titles that you've probably never heard of. There are jobs for people who work as gaffers, grips, and best boys.

Like most young people, you may have dreamed of becoming a movie star so you could be famous and make a lot of money. You've thought of all the fancy cars you could buy and the mansion you could have overlooking the beach with another house in the mountains. Or maybe you would like to be a director and be in charge of the movie production. You have an idea about the kind of movie you would make and who you would want to be in it.

But there are many different kinds of careers in the movies. A professional movie production is a collaboration of many people doing many different kinds of jobs, from seemingly unimportant jobs like running errands and making coffee to big jobs like designing the sets for the movie and keeping the movie within budget. A person who works on a movie production may have a job

Hundreds of people are needed to work on sets of big-budget films like *Cleopatra*.

working on lighting, running the sound equipment, helping with the costumes or wardrobe, or getting the cars that are used in the movie production. There is someone to position the actors in the scene that is being filmed, someone to signal the start of a take, and someone to keep track of what is in each scene so that for tomorrow's shoot the scene has the same things in it. There is someone to build the sets and paint them. There is someone to hold the boom, or microphone, in place and someone to record the sound. Other people make sure that all the departments of the movie production work together and that everybody gets paid.

Who does what on a movie production depends on the size of the production and the production requirements of the movie. Production requirements include all the things that go into making the movie, from how many locations will be used to how many stunts will be needed to how many actors and extras will be in it. As is typical in the movie business, a person's job title does not always tell you exactly what that person does. For example, the set designer does not actually design the sets for the movie production, but rather draws the blueprints or plans for building the sets. The production designer or art director designs the set. A person with the job title of producer may not actually help with the production of the movie but may simply have given money to help get the movie made. Other job titles are even less revealing. The gaffer on the movie is the head of the lighting crew, the best boy is the assistant to the gaffer, and the Foley artist creates sound effects.

Careers in the movies can be categorized by the stages in which a movie is made. Movies are made in stages that go from planning the movie to shooting the movie to editing and final preparation. A movie project begins with the preproduction stage. Then comes the production stage, and finally the postproduction stage.

Preproduction Stage

A movie production starts with a script or an idea for a script. Once a script has the green light, or the go-ahead, the movie production process is started. The producer of a picture heads up a movie project and is the first person to be hired by the movie studio making the picture. Sometimes the producer gets the script first and goes to the studio to get financial backing for making the movie, or makes it as an independent film.

The preproduction stage of making a movie is the planning stage. The producer and director hire the key people who will head the different departments that make the movie. These department heads begin planning their work and hiring their crews. They include the director of photography, the art director or production designer, the music composer, and the film editor. Because a movie is basically a director's vision of how the screenplay should be translated into film, the director tries to ensure that everyone working on the movie has the same idea of how the movie will look. If the movie script is still being developed when the movie is given the go-ahead for production, it is during the preproduction stage that the script is finalized.

The director of photography decides how the movie will be photographed. During preproduction, the director of photography will work on the script with the director to decide on a filming strategy and how large a crew will be needed. The director of photography then hires the other people who will handle the photography and lighting.

The art director will plan what sets will be needed during the preproduction stage. He or she will then hire the rest of the crew, who will build and decorate the sets. The music director or composer will work with the director on what kind of music to use for the movie. He or she will start writing original compositions for the music track or secure the music from other sources. The film editor will work with the director to determine how the film will be edited and how the director wants the movie to look when production is completed. The film editor also hires an editing team during preproduction.

Other crew members are also hired during the preproduction stage. The costume designer will begin designing the costumes and will hire a staff to get costumes from the wardrobe department or to buy or rent them. On major motion pictures, the stars are also hired by the producer and director during the preproduction stage. The casting director will be hired by the producer to get the other actors and film extras that are needed for the movie.

The Production Stage

The production stage is when the movie is actually filmed. Many people are needed during this stage of the film. Actors, stunt people, lighting technicians, sound mixers, costumers, and makeup artists all work during the production stage. Certain jobs in the movies overlap two or more stages of a movie production. The producer and the department heads work through all of the stages. The actors work only during the production stage unless they are brought in later to replace dialogue on the sound track. The lighting technicians and wardrobe assistants also work only during the production stage.

The size and composition of a crew that is hired to work on a movie production will vary depending on the production schedule, that is, what scenes are being filmed and where they are located. The number of people who work on a movie also depends on what kind of a movie it is. If it is an action-adventure film set in many foreign locations, for example, a James Bond–type film, it will require hundreds of people to work on the location shooting. If it is a low-budget film with a small cast and simple sets, the number of crew needed is smaller.

During the production stage, the set crew builds and decorates the sets. The photography and lighting crews position the cameras and the lights to film the scene that is being shot that day. The wardrobe crew helps the actors dress for the scene they are shooting, and then takes care of the costumes once the actors take them off. The stunt crew prepares for the stunts that are being filmed that day.

On a typical day of production, beginning early in the morning, the carpenters will begin building the next set that will be needed for filming. They must have it built before the painters and wall hangers can come in and do their work and the set decorators and dressers can position the furnishings. On the set where the day's filming will take place, the property master will be placing the props that will be used for that day. The lighting technicians will make sure that the lights are positioned correctly and focused. Later, before the scene is actually filmed, the camera assistants will make sure that the cameras are loaded with film. The camera operators will be in place and ready to begin filming. The sound crew will take their places, getting the booms ready to pick up the dialogue of the actors and checking the recording equipment.

Just before a scene is filmed, the wardrobe crew will help the actors get into their costumes. The script continuity person will make sure that the scene is set and that everything is in position according to how it was placed on the previous day. Once the director is ready to begin filming a scene, the assistant director will call for the actors to take their places. When the director calls for action, the cameras start to roll and the actors begin the scene. After the filming is completed, the film is taken by a runner to the film editor who begins processing the film for the dailies. Dailies are the takes from the day that the directors and department heads review to make adjustments or changes for the next day's filming.

In major movie production work, all of the people involved are all members of unions. The actors belong to the Screen Actors Guild. Unions have rules about how long their members can work during a day of filming, how many breaks they must have, and the minimum salary that they must be paid. These rules are all taken into account by the producer and production manager when planning a day's shooting schedule. After all the scenes have been filmed, the movie goes into the post-production stage.

The Postproduction Stage

The camera crews have finished filming the movie. The actors have been released. The sets have been taken down by the strike-crew and the grips. The movie is now in the postproduction stage. The people who work during this stage are trying to get the movie into its final form so that it can be released and distributed to the theaters.

All the movie takes are in and the film editor is working to complete the "rough cut" of the movie. Most of the work during the postproduction stage is done by the film editor and the director. The film editor works with the different takes of the scenes to create the kind of movie the director is trying to make. The director may call in other people to look at the film as it is being edited from the rough cut into the "fine cut."

Once the fine cut is completed, the other postpro-duction work will be done. The sound-effects team adds sound effects. The Foley artists replace sounds from the original filming, such as the sound of an actor's foot-steps as he or she walks down a city street. If there is replacement dialogue to be added to the sound track, the actors are called back to record their dialogue over

Who Works During the Production Stage of a Movie

- Producer
- Director
- Director of Photography
- Art Director/Production Designer
- Music Composer
- Film Editor
- Production Manager
- Production Accountant
- Assistant Director
- Best Boy
- Gaffer
- Key Grip
- Grip
- Lighting Technicians
- Script Supervisor
- Camera Operator
- Camera Assistants
- Still Photographer
- Sound Technicians
- Production Sound Mixer

- Boom Operator
- Art Director
- Carpenters (Prop Makers)
- Set Decorator
- Set Dresser
- Painters
- Wallpaper Hangers
- Drapers
- Costume Designer
- Costumers
- Wardrobe Assistants
- Makeup Artists
- Hair Stylists
- Property Master
- Special Effects Supervisor
- Stunt Coordinator
- Stunt Artists
- Actors
- Film Extras
- Clapper Loader

the original dialogue. Depending on the music that is being added, a conductor and orchestra may be recording the music track during the postproduction stage as the conductor watches the fine cut on a large screen. Once the sound tracks are completed, these are added to the film by the sound mixer.

The fine cut is now shown to test audiences to get their reaction. Any further changes requested by studio executives and producers are made and a "final cut" of the movie is made. The movie is now ready to be released and distributed to movie theaters.

Who Works During the Postproduction Stage of a Movie

- Producer
- Director
- Director of Photography
- Art Director/Production Designer
- Music Composer
- Film Editor
- Sound Effects Editor
- Sound Mixer
- Foley Artists
- Conductor
- Musicians

Other Careers in the Movies

There are some careers related to the movie industry that have little to do with the production stages of making a movie, and you may find these jobs more suitable. They include agents, marketing and promotion people, and entertainment attorneys.

Producers, Directors, and Scriptwriters

3

A movie project begins with the screenplay. When a major motion picture studio or a producer options the rights to a screenplay, the studio or producer is interested in making it into a movie. When they agree to provide the financial backing for it, the production process begins.

The producer, the director, and the scriptwriter are the key people working at the beginning of the production process. A movie project does not begin until a producer is on board. A producer is either hired by a studio to manage a movie production, or the producer brings a screenplay or script idea to a studio for financial backing. The producer hires the director and the two of them often work together to hire the other key people on the project. The other key people are the art director, the director of photography, the film editor, and the music composer. The art director is the head of the set production department. The director of photography is the head of the photography and lighting department. The film editor heads up the film editing department, and the music composer provides the musical score for the sound track.

The Producer

The producer is the first person to be involved with a movie project. Oftentimes, he or she develops the movie project from the beginning by purchasing the rights to a screenplay, a book, a play, or a magazine article, or optioning the rights to tell someone's story. If the movie project starts with the producer, he or she gets a studio interested in making and financing it. The producer also hires the director for a movie project and may help hire the other department heads and the stars and other actors.

The producer follows the movie project from the preproduction to postproduction stage. It is the producer's job to oversee the production of the movie and to make sure that the movie stays within the budget. The producer has a say in many of the decisions that are made about the movie and works with the department heads during filming. He or she checks in with the accountant to see how the production is going and must approve all major expenditures. The person in charge of day-to-day production, who is on-site as the movie is filming, and reports to the producer on how it is going, is the production manager.

Because the producer is in charge of getting the movie made, he or she has the most responsibility for how well the movie does at the box office. If it is successful at the box office, meaning that a lot of people go to see the movie and it makes a lot of money, the producer gets credit for the movie's success. If the movie does poorly at the box office or loses money, the producer is the first one to be blamed for the failure of the project.

There are different kinds of producers, depending on the size of a movie and its budget. A line producer is a production manager, hiring the heads of the various production departments. An executive producer is often the person who comes up with the money for the film. Some people may have the title of producer or executive producer but have little to do with the actual production of the movie.

The producer has to know about getting a story made, about budgets and salaries, and about how the many people who work together on a movie get the job done. The producer has to be able to get the best work out of everybody on the staff and crew. The producer has to be familiar with story ideas and what makes a good story. Producers must know bookkeeping and accounting, and must have managerial skills and be able to motivate people to do a good job.

To become a producer, attending a college film production program will provide the education and training to help you get started. You can also attend a theater arts program and take courses in accounting, bookkeeping, and English literature. You can also get production training in video and television before working on a movie production.

Once you have the education, you should try to get a job on a production crew doing anything from being a runner to working as a production assistant. By observation and by visiting other areas of the movie production, you will see what other people do. If you get a job reading and reporting on story material for an agent or studio, you will learn more about movie scripts and what makes a script a good prospect for a successful movie. The key to getting started as a producer is to learn all production work and budgeting, and how to evaluate story material.

The Director

Lights! Camera! Action! This is the director's job—to call the movie production crews and actors into action. Usually when you think of who is in charge of making a movie, you think of the director. It is the director who is the creative guide. He or she decides how the screenplay will be interpreted and made into a movie. The director's interpretation includes how the lighting, sound, camera work, sets, costumes, and music are used to enhance the story, not to mention telling the actors how to play their parts. All these elements help to make up a director's style and allow audiences to recognize a movie as a certain director's work.

The director is responsible for the way the movie looks. The director is hired by the producer during the preproduction stage of the film. The director, with the producer's help, decides who should be hired as the director of photography, the art director, and the film editor. During preproduction, the director works with these department heads to plan the production requirements of the movie.

To establish a career as a director in Hollywood, you need a successful film project to get you started. Because a director has so much say in how a screenplay is interpreted, and because movies are so expensive to make, studio executives want to know that their director has the talent and vision to make a movie that people will want to see. The executives of major studios are not the people to go to for your first break. Most feature films in Hollywood are directed by experienced directors, those who have a proven track record of getting a picture made on budget, on time, and with box office success.

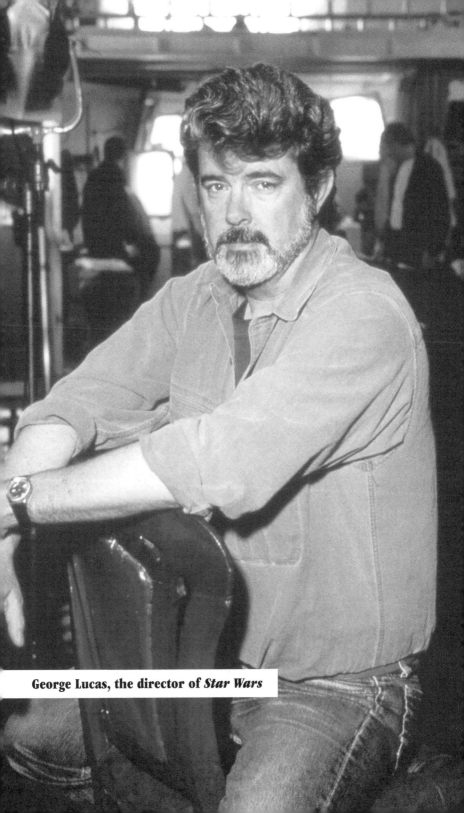

George Lucas, the director of *Star Wars*

To become a director you will have to go to a film school and major in film production. The best programs are those from which you will graduate with a completed film project, something to show what you can do. Once you have completed your education, the more you know about film production, the better. By working as an assistant director, you will gain practical experience. Working on small independent film projects or in television will also help you to get directing experience.

The more directing experience you have, the better your résumé will look and the more examples you will have of your work. Sometimes the only way to get started as a director is to develop and finance your own film projects. This is what many young film students end up doing. As the technical aspects of filmmaking become easier to master with less expensive equipment, from video cameras to computer editing systems, it has become possible to make a full-length movie on a limited budget.

To be a director, you need to be technically oriented, theatrically inclined, a writer, a graphic artist, a poet, a philosopher, and a mechanic. You have to know what makes a good story and you must be well read. You have to keep up-to-date on what people are seeing and what they are interested in. You have to be able to supervise and motivate large numbers of crew and actors. The best-known directors are strong-willed and charismatic, and have the respect of their crew.

There may be several assistant directors on a movie production. The assistants work with the director to help instruct the actors. Some of the duties of an assistant director include rehearsing the scenes with the actors before filming begins and supervising when the crews strike the sets.

The Scriptwriter

Got an idea for a movie? Most people do. Sometimes you have an idea that seems just right for a movie. Or maybe you have seen a movie lately that made you think you could write something better. Or maybe you saw something in the news that made you think, "That is a great idea for a movie!" That is pretty much how the idea for a movie script begins. Scriptwriters make a living by turning their ideas or other people's ideas into screenplays.

Working as a scriptwriter in Hollywood seems like a very glamorous job. From the entertainment shows, magazines, and award ceremonies, it looks like a job where you socialize with the stars and make a lot of money. If you are really lucky, you may even win an Academy Award for best screenplay for all your hard work. What an exciting career that would be!

As an established Hollywood scriptwriter, you do have the opportunity to make a lot of money for a writing project, much more than newspaper reporters or freelance magazine writers can earn. A scriptwriter who has written a successful screenplay can make anywhere from $100,000 to $250,000 for one screenplay. But for every screenplay that is made into a movie, there are thousands that never make it off the shelf of the studio executive's office.

The Writers Guild of America, the union that scriptwriters belong to, reported in 1995 that of the 8,000 members, only 4,000 reported income from writing in any given year. The average yearly income for a guild member was $50,000. Not quite 400 guild members made over $1 million in 1995; not a very high percentage out of 8,000. A very small number of well-established scriptwriters got a percentage of the box office receipts. But it is the possibility of making that million dollars for one script that is appealing to many young writers.

To work as a scriptwriter, you can be involved in a movie project in different ways. One way to get a script made into a movie is to write an original script that gets purchased by a producer or a studio. To get a script read by a story analyst at a Hollywood studio today, you will have to have a literary agent. Most studios accept scripts submitted only from agents to protect themselves legally. In the past, studios have been sued by writers who claimed that the studio stole their ideas after the script submitted to the studio was rejected. Getting an agent will require that you submit a completed screenplay to provide the agent an example of your writing ability. Even when you get an agent, this does not guarantee that your movie will get purchased or optioned by a movie studio.

Another way to work as a scriptwriter in Hollywood is to work for a studio or a producer. When the story analyst who reads scripts for a movie studio recommends a book to a studio executive as a good option for a movie, the studio executive will hire a scriptwriter to adapt the book into a screenplay. Studios also hire scriptwriters to do rewrites on scripts that have been purchased from other scriptwriters. Usually these writers have experience and the producer knows their ability to make a script work on film.

Writers can also be hired by a producer to develop a script. The producer may have a script idea that he or she wants developed into a full-length script. The producer may have bought the rights to a treatment—a description of an idea for development into a screenplay—that is to be turned into a script. The producer may have bought the rights to adapt a novel or play into a movie or bought the rights to make someone's life story into a movie for television or the big screen.

Sometimes a script starts out as a concept that a writer pitches to the studio executive. A concept is a few sentences or pages on what the movie is about. It is just enough to give the studio executive or producer an idea of what the movie will be like. If he or she likes it, he or she may ask for a treatment, a longer version of the concept where the idea for the movie is expanded on in greater detail. If the studio executive likes the treatment, he or she may option it for a movie. This means that the treatment will be developed into a full-length script. But the original scriptwriter may not be hired to write the script. It could be given to another scriptwriter, someone whom the studio has worked with before or who has written successful screenplays. Studio executives and producers want to work with a sure thing. They like to hire writers that they know can produce the script in a timely manner and in workable form. Oftentimes a treatment written by a new writer will be given to one of these writers to develop into the full-length script.

If the original writer is commissioned to write the script, then the writer will be paid for turning the concept or treatment into a full-length script. After completing the script, the writer turns it in to the movie executive for consideration. Even then, being paid to write the full-length script is no guarantee that the script will be made into a movie. The studio has the right to turn down the script project at any time. Studio executives are in the business of getting movies made. They hear movie pitches every week from agents and producers as they look for the next big blockbuster movie script. They

Scriptwriters are often asked to make changes to the script while filming is in progress.

have hundreds of movie scripts sent to them every week from agents and producers, and they are tough to please.

Once the script is written, the producer, director, or studio executives may request changes to it. Even as the movie is being filmed, an actor may want certain lines changed or may have problems with the script as it is written. The scriptwriter may be asked to make changes while the filming is in progress. The scriptwriter must be willing to meet these demands and make the necessary changes.

Studios used to pay to option the rights to many projects just so they would have them and another studio wouldn't. They did this with the understanding that not all of these scripts would be made into movies. Because of increased costs and tighter budgets, studios are much more selective in the scripts they option and do not option as many as before. As a result, there are fewer opportunities for a scriptwriter to be commissioned to develop a full-length script. As a scriptwriter, you may have a screenplay purchased by a studio only to have it stalled in the production process. It may get passed along to a writer hired by the studio, go through a series of rewrites, and never get made. Sometimes the studio executive will change his or her mind about the script and decide not to make it into a movie.

There are hundreds of new movies that come out of Hollywood every year. Out of this number, there are thousands of scripts sent to studios and agents that never get made into movies. Scriptwriting is a tough, highly competitive business.

Other Opportunities for Scriptwriting

There are more opportunities in scriptwriting today than there were a few years ago. With the increase in cable channels and made-for-TV movies, the market for movie scripts has expanded. For example, the programming for HBO and Showtime now includes several original movies. A few years ago, these channels only included movies that had been in theaters first. Today the cable channels are competing for good original scripts along with major studios.

There has also been an increase in movies that are made directly for the video market. More and more animated, action-adventure, and horror films are made to be sent directly to the video store and are never shown at movie theaters. A third area of increase in movie markets is the foreign film market. Feature films are often made as a collaboration between a Hollywood studio and a foreign distributor and sent directly to the foreign film audience.

Because of an increase in these markets for feature films, there are more opportunities for the scriptwriter to sell original screenplays. A scriptwriter can also work for a corporation or large company. Businesses use movies for training programs, for educational videos, or to promote company products.

To have a career as a scriptwriter, you do not have to have anything more than a talent for writing scripts. But getting a college degree in English, film, or creative writing will give you the background you need as a writer. Attending a film program that emphasizes scriptwriting will give you the training to write scripts in the correct format. Depending on the program, you may get your script made into a film project.

Acting and Stunt Work

It is probably every young person's dream at one time or another to be a star. It looks like a fabulous lifestyle when you see photos of stars in magazines. Who wouldn't want to be a movie star and have a glamorous lifestyle and all the money that goes with it?

Thousands of young people go to Hollywood every year with that same dream, to try to make it in the movies. You have probably heard stories of a person getting discovered while working as a waiter in a restaurant. A Hollywood casting agent was at the restaurant one day and told the wanna-be star that he or she had just the look that was needed for a new movie role. Or a producer came in for lunch who was casting a movie and said, "I have a part that would be just right for you." That rarely happens. Your chances of getting discovered like this in Hollywood are probably as good as winning the lottery some day. It could happen, but the odds are against it.

To become a working actor in the movies takes determination and a lot of hard work. The reason you hear about people working as waiters while trying to get work as actors is because most people must have other jobs to support themselves while they are trying to break in to the movie business. To get work in the movies, particularly in Hollywood, you have to go to many auditions and learn to accept rejection without becoming discouraged.

Many careers are helped by someone who knows someone who gets you an interview or knows about a place that is hiring. That is definitely true in Hollywood. The best way to get a job on a major movie production as an actor is to know somebody. Much of the movie business really is about who you know. Many production jobs are obtained because somebody knows somebody or is related to somebody.

It may not seem like you know anybody who is working in the movie business, but maybe you do without realizing it. One way to find a contact is to ask around. There may be someone from your hometown or school who is working in the film industry, maybe not as an actor but doing some kind of production work. If your cousin's friend is working as a film animator, he or she may know someone else who can introduce you to a casting agent or a producer. Or the cousin's friend may know about a movie project under development and who to contact to get an audition for it. Another way to make contacts is through a college alumni association. By attending a college theater arts program, you will get not only an education in performing, but you will learn about others from the school who have gone on with their acting careers.

To be an actor in the movies you usually have to build a career gradually. This means going to many auditions and taking small parts wherever you can find them. You may start out as a film extra with no lines at all. Most film extras have nonspeaking roles—for instance, the person at the next table in the restaurant scene with his or her back to the camera, turned away from the star. But this is a way to get experience and to make more contacts. The next role you get may have only one line. After waiting on tables hoping for your big break, you may wind up on film as the waiter in the restaurant serving the star.

All movies are cast by casting directors, who will hire only actors who have an agent. You can contact agents directly. A list of agents is available from the Screen Actors Guild, the union for actors. When you have an agent, it is the agent's job to get you auditions. He or she must keep up on which movies and casting directors are holding auditions and try to get auditions for the people he or she represents.

For any audition, you will need what every casting or talent agent will want to see, a headshot and a résumé. A headshot is a black-and-white, 8 1/2-by-11 photograph of yourself. Some photographers specialize in these kinds of photos, or a talent agency will be able to recommend a photographer. The résumé should include acting experience, education, and training. It is also a good idea to have a video of your acting performance from a play, a commercial, or some other production. If you don't have this video, you can have a video made of yourself doing a monologue or acting in a scene with another actor. To prepare for auditions, you should also have a monologue ready because a casting director may ask you to do one at an audition.

To work as an actor in Hollywood you must belong to the Screen Actors Guild. One way to get into the Screen

Actors Guild is to get offered a movie role. Then you pay your fee and you are in the guild. The best way to get work as an actor is to do any kind of acting you can. Acting in a theater production will get you roles to add to your résumé. If you can get work in a commercial, it pays well and is something to add to your résumé.

If you want to work as an actor in a major motion picture, you will probably have to live in Los Angeles. That is where the opportunities are. But you can work in the movies in other cities, too, like New York or Chicago. The newspapers in a major city will list auditions that are being held for local productions or movies that are being filmed on location. This will usually require getting a talent agent, whose job it is to get you auditions.

Although some young people head straight for Hollywood when they get out of high school, many others go to college and get a bachelor's degree in theater arts first. Going through a theater program will give you training and experience. You will get to be in productions and have roles to put on your résumé. Also, you will have something to fall back on if you decide to pursue something other than acting, especially if you earn a minor in another area or have coursework that prepares you for other work.

Film Extras

When you see a scene in a movie where the principal actors walk through a shopping mall, the other people who are there are not ordinary people out shopping. These are the film extras, and they are part of the movie cast, too. Any time that there is a large number of people

Many film actors start their careers in the theater.

in a movie scene, such as a crowd scene, these people are film extras. Film extras are actors who work in the movies in nonspeaking roles. Some extras specialize by performing certain roles on a regular basis, such as portraying someone who is in the military. They may even have their own costumes. To get work as a film extra, you have to go to auditions that specify they are casting for film extras.

Some film extras get work on movies through the Central Casting Corporation. This organization categorizes actors by type. A casting director will make a request for extras by type and numbers needed and the actors are called to work on the film for a day or an afternoon.

Stunt Artists

Have you ever wanted to leap from a burning building, or roll a car in a car chase, or fall down a flight of stairs, and never get hurt? People who work as stunt artists are required to do these things as part of their job. This is what they get paid for, to take risks and to perform certain dangerous acts in the movies and make them look believable.

It might seem that a person who does this kind of work would be someone who likes to take risks, a daredevil type who is always pushing the edge and putting himself or herself in life-threatening situations. But this is not the case for the stunt artist. Stunts that are part of a movie script are carefully planned by the stunt coordinator and the stunt artist. They are set up using special effects and illusions, similar to those used by a magician, to make the stunts look real and believable. The stunts are set up so that the stunt artist suffers as little risk as possible. Some stunt artists specialize in certain kinds of stunts because of the skills they have, like sword fighting or swimming. Stunt artists are in good physical shape and use skill and preparation to perform their stunts.

Stunt artists may work in the movies as doubles for the stars and principal actors. When the script calls for a star to do something dangerous or something the star does not want to do, the stunt double is called in to perform the action. The film that is shot of the stunt double is edited into the movie scene so that you cannot tell that it is a stunt double and not the star performing the action. Stunt doubles and body doubles resemble an actor in physical size. In the movie *Mission: Impossible II*, when Tom Cruise is riding the motorcycle in the dangerous chase scenes toward the end of the movie, some of the shots are of a stunt double. But when you watch the movie, it looks like Tom Cruise in every shot.

A stunt double is used instead of the actor for several reasons. Stars are considered to be too valuable to a movie production to be placed at risk. If something happens to the star while filming, it could slow the entire production down or bring it to a halt altogether. This is a costly situation. Equipment may have been rented for a location shoot, crew members are on union time and have to be paid, and there is a schedule to follow to get the movie made. The stars also have insurance on themselves and the insurance may require that they not take certain risks in their movie roles. A star's contract will spell out what the star is or is not willing to do for the role he or she is playing. Sometimes the star does not wish to be seen in partial or full nudity. If he or she wants to do the role, a body double will be used to stand in for the actor during scenes that require nudity.

What skills and abilities does a person have to have to be a stunt artist? He or she may have special physical abilities, like the ability to box for a role as a sparring partner in a boxing scene, or the ability to ride a horse. Stunt people must be able to work well under pressure. Action sequences requiring stunts are expensive to shoot and require meticulous setup. There is a lot of pressure to shoot the scene in one take, to get it right the first time. A stunt person must be able to stay focused and use his or her special skills to get the job done right the first time. Stunt artists also work long hours and in difficult conditions, from extreme heat to extreme cold to difficult costuming. To work as a stunt artist, you must be prepared for the long days and strenuous work that go with it.

Most stunt people get their training to perform stunts on the job. Some begin as assistants to other stunt people or get mentored by stunt coordinators. Stunt people will go to movie sets where stunts are being performed to observe how others work and learn this way. If you want to get started as a stunt artist, having a special skill is a good way to get that first job. You must also be prepared to start in some other area of production work, as a runner or assistant to a stunt crew, to learn about stunt work and the movie business.

Like most careers in the movies, stunt artists belong to a union. The first job you get will get you into the union. You are then required to pay union dues. Once in the union, you are guaranteed a certain daily or weekly wage for your work, which is called scale.

The Stunt Coordinator

It is the stunt coordinator's job to set up the stunts for the movie. The stunt coordinator works with the director during the preproduction stage of the movie to determine what stunts are called for in the script and how they will be set up. The stunt coordinator then works with the special effects coordinator and property master to determine what props will be needed for the stunts, like firearms or other special equipment. The stunt coordinator prepares a budget to estimate how many people will be needed for the stunts and then hires stunt artists.

During the production stage of the movie, the stunt coordinator works with the director and the stunt artists to set up the stunts. They will determine what the best camera angles to use are, both to achieve the effect they want for the stunt, and also to insure the safety of the stunt artists.

To get a job as a stunt coordinator, you have to first work as a stunt artist. The coordinator must know how stunts can be performed and what risks are involved for the stunt artist. You must also be able to look at a script and determine how a stunt can be performed based on what the scriptwriter has written. You have to turn the written word into an exciting, believable scene in a movie. For all this hard work, the successful stunt coordinator can earn a six-figure yearly income.

Photography and Lighting

5

The people who film the movie are part of the photography crew. They determine how the scene will be photographed, set up the camera angles for each scene, operate the cameras, and keep them in focus and loaded with film. Careers in this field include the director of photography, the camera operators, and the camera assistants.

A movie scene cannot be filmed without special lighting and equipment. The photography crew also sets up the lights for each scene, focuses the lights, sets up and keeps track of the power cables, and helps to move the dollies and cranes that the camera operators ride on. The people who work on the camera crew include the gaffer, the lighting technicians, the key grip, the grip, and the best boy.

The Director of Photography

The director of photography, also called the cinematographer, has the job of photographing the movie. He or

The director of photography, or cinematographer, photographs the movie.

she is in charge of the overall quality of the photography and how the movie will look visually. Together, the director and the director of photography determine how the movie script will be translated into the visual medium.

The director of photography is hired by the producer or the director. Like the film editor, he or she is someone whose work the director knows or who has been recommended to the director. Usually the director of photography has several years of experience in film or video work. He or she has worked her way up from a camera assistant or some other film work.

The director of photography goes through the script, scene by scene, to plan how to position the cameras for each scene and what lighting to use to achieve the desired visual effect. What kind of lighting is used depends on whether the script calls for an interior scene or an exterior scene. It also depends on how the director wants the scene to feel, or the emotional tone he or she wants to come across.

To work as a director of photography, or in any capacity as part of the photography or lighting crew, you have to think visually. You have to be able to interpret the written word of the movie script into the visual medium. The director of photography also knows camera work, camera angles, lenses, the filming requirements of different locations, and how to work with a director to achieve the look the director wants for the film.

To become a director of photography on a major motion picture takes years of experience and work on many productions as an assistant or on the camera crew. It is a position few people achieve because of the demand for quality work and the small number of productions. The best way to earn a director of photography credit is to work your way up in the film business or work on smaller productions and independent films.

The Camera Operator

The camera operator runs the camera during the shooting of the movie. He or she works under the direction of the director of photography. The director of photography has planned how the scene will be filmed and where to position the camera. The key grip has set up the camera as instructed by the gaffer. The lighting has been positioned by the lighting technicians. The scene is ready to be filmed. The director of photography instructs the camera operator on where to focus the camera while shooting the take, whether it's a long shot, a medium shot, or a close-up. This is planned out in advance of the scene. The camera crew also works with headsets so they can communicate with one another while filming and make adjustments to camera angles, focus, and so on. When there are several cameras operating at one time during the filming of a picture, the chief camera operator is the supervisor of the other camera operators.

Running a camera is not as easy as it looks. The motion picture camera is large and sits on a tripod. The camera operator must stand for long periods of time. Occasionally, video work may require the camera operator to carry a video camera around. This technique is mostly used in television. Sometimes the camera operator must sit or stand on dollies that follow the action of the actors. The dollies may move up and down or be high off the ground for the camera to make long shots. The camera may also shoot from a small airplane or helicopter for aerial shots.

To work as a camera operator, you must be skilled as a photographer. You must understand camera angles and lighting and be able to work with a camera that may be moving or on a crane. Attending film school and specializing in movie photography will give you the training you need to be a camera operator. You will probably have to start in the movie business as a camera assistant.

The Camera Assistant

The camera assistant adjusts the lens of the camera during the shooting of a movie scene as needed for the camera operator. He or she also loads the camera with film and assists the camera operator as needed. A motion picture camera is a large piece of equipment. As a camera operator, you cannot easily reach around the camera to adjust the focus. As the camera operator focuses on the scene and moves in for a close-up or pulls back for a long shot, the camera assistant adjusts the lens to keep the camera in focus.

The Stills Photographer

The stills photographer or unit photographer is the person who takes pictures of the cast and crew during the production of the movie. The stills photographer takes pictures with a regular 35-mm camera, not a motion picture camera. The stills photographer works with the camera operator and takes pictures of the set during filming to document the filming of the scene. The stills photographer also takes pictures of the actors and the production in progress. The photographs are released to the media for publicity purposes. The stills photographer must be able to take pictures that re-create the feel of the movie. If the director has a dark look to the scenes, as in the *Batman* movies, the photographs must also look this way.

Careers in Lighting

When you watch a movie scene, you don't usually think about the lighting. You may notice if you are watching an indoor scene or an outdoor scene, if it is daylight or nighttime, but you don't think about how it got that way. To make a movie look natural to the movie audience, special lighting is required to photograph each scene. Lighting is necessary because a camera lens is not as sophisticated as the naked eye. You have to add light to make a scene look as it would appear in a natural setting. It is the lighting crew's job to set up and focus the lighting for the movie production.

People who work on the lighting crew position the lights for the scene, focus the lights, add special lighting equipment like scrims, or diffusing materials, to adjust the intensity of the lights, remove or cover up things in the scene that cause glare or reflect too much light, and locate the electrical sources to power the lighting equipment.

The people who work on lighting in a movie production work on technical or nontechnical jobs. Technical people work on electrical tasks and work with the gaffer. People who work on nontechnical tasks work as grips. Careers in this field include the gaffer, the lighting technician, the grip, including the key grip, the best boy, the standby painter, and the nursery man.

The Gaffer

The gaffer is in charge of the lighting crew. He or she works with the director of photography from the start of production. Because the director of photography must be free to work with the director and the camera operator to set up the shots, the gaffer acts as the go-between between the director of photography and the lighting crew. The gaffer determines what lights will be needed at the locations where filming will take place and what lighting is available at the location. The gaffer makes sure that the lighting equipment needed for the various locations is ordered and there to use. The gaffer also hires the lighting crew needed for the location shoots, the grips, best boy, and lighting technicians. In general, he or she is responsible for seeing that the technical aspects of the location shooting go smoothly.

To work as a gaffer you must have training and experience as a lighting technician, that is, you must be highly skilled in electrical and lighting work. Usually a gaffer has worked his or her way up from other jobs on the lighting crew, such as lighting technician or grip. You also must be organized and able to supervise others.

The Lighting Technician

The lighting technician on a movie set is also called an electrician, but the lighting technician is not like the electricians who work on your home, fixing the wiring, or adding wiring to a new building. The lighting technician on a movie set locates the source of electricity that will power the lighting equipment for the movie shoot.

He or she will "patch in" to that source with the film crew's fuse box to make electricity available for the lighting equipment. If there is no electricity available, the lighting technician will set up an electrical generator to create an electrical source for the location shooting.

The lighting technicians are also the lamp operators. As lamp operators, they "rig," or put, the lights into position for a shoot as instructed by the gaffer. The gaffer will ask the lamp operator or electrician for a particular kind of light or lamp. The operator will put it in place, raise it or lower it, then wait for orders from the gaffer about when to turn it on. The lighting technician focuses the light and adjusts the intensity of the light by adding scrims, or adjusting the metal shutters, called barn doors.

Lighting technicians have special skills and training in electrical work. To work as a lighting technician on a movie you will want to get training from a technical training program as an electrician. You could also attend a college technical theater program where you would receive training on lighting and production work. Like most careers in the movies, you will have to work your way up, as a grip or assistant on the lighting crew, to become a lighting technician.

The Best Boy

The best boy assists the gaffer. He or she orders the lighting equipment needed for the different location shoots and also keeps the paperwork needed for the lighting crew, such as employee time cards. The best boy also runs errands between the production office and the set. This person takes care of the business that the gaffer does not have time to do.

Key Grip, Grip, Dolly Grip, Standby Painter, Nursery Man

All the lights from a scene will have to be moved once filming on that set or location is completed. This is the job of the key grip. The key grip sets up the cameras and moves them. The key grip also runs the crane for the camera and camera operator. The grip moves cables needed to connect the lighting equipment to the power source, and watches the cables to be sure that they stay clear of the dollies when the camera cart is moving. The dolly is run by the dolly grip. The dolly grip moves the crane up and down. If the crane needs to move back and forth, a different grip does this to keep within union rules. This grip sits in what is called the hot seat, a chair next to the crane driver's chair that faces in the opposite direction.

Also part of the lighting crew is the standby painter. If the director of photography determines that an object is reflecting too much light, it is the standby painter's job to add paint to the object to take away the glare. The nursery man's job is to cover up objects that shouldn't be seen in a shot. Oftentimes this means plants or greenery, which is where the job title of "nursery man" comes from.

Education and Training

Work on the lighting crew, particularly as a lighting technician, requires training and skill. An interest in math, science, and electrical circuitry and electronics are good indicators of an interest in a career in lighting.

An artistic flair is also helpful. You have to be able to make power usage computations and be able to repair your equipment.

A vocational technical program that offer courses in electronics and electrical work is a good place to start training for a career in lighting. Obtaining a college degree in technical theater also provides training in lighting and lighting design. You can also get experience by working as an electrician's apprentice, as an electrician's helper for a theater group, or by volunteering at a community theater. It is also a good idea to stay ahead of technical advances in lighting equipment and products by reading magazines and other reference sources on the movie industry.

Most lighting crew members are hired at union scale. The top positions, like the gaffer and key grip, negotiate their own salary for the shoot.

Set Design

The set is the physical world in which the film action takes place. It is the place that was created for Luke Skywalker as a little boy. It is the lab in *Jurassic Park* where the dinosaur eggs are incubating. The set is a place, real or made-up, present time, past, or future, that is built to provide the background for the action and actors in the movie production. The sets are designed and made by people who work on the set crew: the production designer/art director, the set designer, carpenters, set decorator, set dresser, and property master.

To work in set design, you must think visually; that is, you must understand how things will look before they exist. You must be able to work as part of a team that is creating the physical world of the set out of the movie script.

The Art Director/ Production Designer

The head of the set design department is the art director, who is sometimes called the production designer.

The art director presents sketches of the sets to the film director.

The art director is in charge of the visual look of the picture. The art director's job is to design sets for the movie that look authentic and believable. When you are watching the movie, your attention should be drawn to the actors and the story that is being told, not to what the set looks like. The art director's job is to design a set that you don't notice when you are watching the movie.

The art director is like the architect of the set design crew. In fact, many art directors have architecture degrees or training. He or she is responsible for all the physical aspects of the set. Besides designing the way the sets will look, if a location calls for a plane that has crash-landed in the top of a tree, the art director must figure out how to do that.

The art director's job begins during the preproduction stage of the movie. He or she is hired by the director of the movie. Together they will determine the look of the sets based on the time the movie takes place and the style of the movie. The art director may draw sketches of the sets to show to the director as he or she works on the designs.

As an art director, you have to know what colors and kinds of materials to use in the building of the sets. Sometimes the art director works with the costume designer in choosing colors for the costumes that work with the colors of the sets to create a particular effect or tone for the movie. The art director also works with the director of photography in designing the sets. The set construction may require that cameras be placed at certain angles for filming the scene. The art director has to take this into account when designing a set.

The art director hires the main crew that will work on the designing and building of the sets, including the set designer, the set decorator, the set dresser, and the construction coordinator. Although the construction coordinator supervises the construction of the sets, the art director is in charge of building them. He or she will walk through a set as it is being built to make sure that the construction is made according to the plans and that the plans are working to create the type of set the director has requested.

Once filming begins on a set, the art director attends the dailies, the daily screenings of the movie, to check for problems with the set that may show up in the filming. This allows any problems to be fixed before the next day's filming. The art director has assistant art directors to help with the many duties of the set design work.

The Set Designer

Set designer is one of those job titles in the movies that does not actually describe what the person does. The set designer is more like a draftsperson than an actual designer. He or she draws the blueprints for the set that have been designed by the art director. The set designer is also expected to expand on the art director's ideas. He or she drafts the blueprints from the designs and modifies or makes improvements to them. To work as a set designer you must have training in drafting blueprints for theatrical or movie sets.

Carpenters and Prop Makers

Once the set has been designed by the art director and the blueprints have been drafted by the set designer,

Careers in the Movies

somebody has to build the set. That is the job of the carpenters or prop makers.

Members of the set construction crew work long hours. They must work ahead of the other people on the crew, like the painters and the set decorators, because the set must be built before any further work can be done. The set construction crew must also work on deadline. While another scene is being filmed, the next set that will be needed for filming must be built and ready for filming.

The construction coordinator oversees the carpenters. He or she supervises the construction of the set on a daily basis. The construction coordinator reports to the art director about how the set construction is progressing. The art director visits the set construction site as it is being constructed to make sure that it is being built according to plan and that it is going to work for the film.

The carpenters or prop makers do the actual building of the sets. They come in early in the morning and work long hours to get the work done. They must have the set structure built so that the painters, wallpaper hangers, and drapery hangers can come in and do their work. The set must be decorated and furnished by the set decorator. All this work must be completed on schedule so that the director of photography and the director can come in to see how they are going to shoot the next scene. Then the lighting and camera crew will be able to come in and position the lights and cameras for filming.

Carpenters or prop makers who work on a movie production are regular carpenters by trade. They also are skilled in special techniques for set building. Sets are made of special materials, like flats or wood frames covered in muslin. A room may not be finished completely; a wall or ceiling may be left out because you don't see it during the filming. This makes the construction quicker, less expensive, and easier to strike, or tear down. It also allows the director of photography to use more varied camera angles for shooting the scenes on the set.

Once the shooting on a set is completed, a crew comes in and strikes the set. But this is not the carpenters' job. Another crew, called the strike crew, does this. The carpenters are already at work building the next set.

The Set Decorator

The set decorator dresses the set. Working with the art director, he or she chooses the furnishings, drapes, and accessories for the set. The set decorator has interior design training and experience and knows how to work with color and furnishings to create the mood that the director wants for a particular set design. The set decorator works with the art director to select colors and themes to use for dressing the set. The set decorator must make the set look like a real place. Even if it is a place in the future or a science-fiction setting, the set must look authentic. It must look like a real place where people would live or real action would take place.

The set decorator usually has an assistant set decorator, sometimes called the lead man. The assistant set decorator, or lead man, "takes the lead" in getting objects and artifacts that will be used to decorate the set. The set decorator will decide what items are needed. When the assistant set decorator locates items to use for the set, he or she will take pictures of the objects to show to the set decorator for approval before purchasing or renting the items. On large productions where many objects and artifacts are needed or where the sets are elaborate, there is a large crew of people who get all the objects needed. Once all the items have been located, the set dresser has the job of arranging the items for the shoot.

The Property Master

Properties are all the extra things that are used in a scene that are not part of the set or the location. For example, if the set is a teenager's bedroom that has a desk with a CD player on it, the items on the desk, like the computer, pencils and paper, and the CD player are considered properties, or props. If the set is in a school cafeteria where lunch is being served, the food trays, food, straws, and napkin holders are all props for the scene. It is the property master's job to get the properties that are needed for each scene.

The property master reads through the script to make a list of what props are needed for each scene. Props are obtained from the studio's properties department or rented or purchased from theatrical supply companies, secondhand stores, or specialty shops that have hard-to-find items like antiques. There are usually assistants in the properties department to help the property master with these tasks and to place the props at the start of each scene and strike them from the scene when shooting is finished.

Training and Education

To prepare for a career with the set design crew you must be able to design, draw, and decorate. The best preparation for a career in set design is a bachelor of arts degree from a theater arts program that has a strong program in set design. This kind of program teaches a person how to interpret the written word visually. When you read something, you have to be able to picture it in your mind. With a theater arts education, you learn the skills needed to put what you visualize when reading the movie script into plans, blueprints, models, and sketches. Other degree programs to consider are fine arts, graphic arts, or illustration. If you want to be a production designer or art director, the best preparation is a bachelor of arts degree in art or architecture and a master of fine arts degree in theater arts. In general, to make it in the highly competitive area of set design, you will need new ideas and a lot of talent. Even with the necessary education and training, you will likely have to start at the entry level on a movie production. Your first job may be as a runner or making coffee. By observing the work of the others on the set design crew and asking questions, you can learn more about their jobs and make contacts for further work.

Costuming

7

The costumes in a movie may be breathtakingly beautiful, like the lavish gowns and jeweled dresses that Drew Barrymore wore in *Ever After*, or they can be simple, like the one Anakin Skywalker wore in *Star Wars, Episode One*. The costumes in a movie production, their style, the colors and fabric that are used to make them, and the way they are accessorized are the responsibility of the costume and makeup department. The costumes and the people who work on them are as important to a movie production as the lighting or the set design.

Every person who is in a movie must appear in costume. Everyone must be dressed according to the style of the picture. If the film is set in sixteenth-century Europe, like the Drew Barrymore movie *Ever After*, you cannot have an extra in the movie who is wearing tennis shoes. Even if it is a crowd scene and a long shot so that the camera is filming far away from the crowd and you can't really see people's feet, the tennis shoes would take away from the authenticity of the picture. The costuming helps to give the movie the authentic look that the director is trying to achieve. The hairstyling and makeup complete the look and are part of the costuming effect.

A period piece, such as the film *Gladiator*, must have costumes for its characters that are historically correct.

The costuming is an important part of how you respond to a movie. What colors an actor is wearing, or what kind of fabric the costumes are made of, all help to create an emotional reaction. If an actor is dressed in a leather jacket, you have one response to him or her. If the actor is dressed in a powder blue tuxedo, you have a different kind of reaction. Costuming helps determine character for the actor. The costuming also contributes to what makes a movie believable and successful at the box office.

Careers in costuming and makeup for movies include the costume designer; the person who helps make the costumes, known as the costumer; the wardrobe assistant, who helps the actors to put on the costumes; and the people who do their hair, or the hairstylists. The people who apply makeup to the actors are the makeup artists.

The Costume Designer

The costume designer is hired by the producer or the director. The costume designer is in charge of the look and style of the clothing for the movie production. He or she designs the original costumes for the movie. Not all the clothing in a movie may be from original designs. Depending on the style or time period of the movie, some clothes may be rented or purchased, but it is the designer's job to determine what the clothes should look like. The costume designer begins working during the preproduction stage of the movie. He or she studies the script, the period and the setting of the film, then draws colored sketches for the director to look at. A successful career as a costume designer is built after earning a reputation for talent and outstanding creative work over years of experience. To be a costume designer you must have design training from a college fine arts program or a design institute. Once you have the education and training, you will likely have to start as a wardrobe assistant or a costumer. If you have exceptional talent, you may get your chance to design costumes for a movie.

The Costumer

Once the costume designer has planned the costuming and wardrobe needs of the actors, the costumer helps construct or sew original costumes for the actors. On larger productions there is a costume crew to make the costumes. The costumer, or costume master, also collects costumes from the studio wardrobe department and costume rental companies, and gets them fitted. Once production begins, the costumer helps the actors get into their costumes. During the production, the costumer takes care of the costumes, hanging them up, getting them mended as needed, and making sure they get laundered.

To be a costumer, you must be skilled in costume and wardrobe construction. This is a specialized kind of sewing. Costumes are not made like street clothes. Costumes require special techniques and skills for the kind of clothing that is to be made. You may have to make undergarments, like corsets, or military uniforms of a special kind. You must also be able to work on certain kinds of sewing equipment, like sergers, and special costume construction equipment.

A degree from a technical theater arts program will help prepare you to work as a costumer. Fashion and design programs will also provide you with training for costume work. Getting practical experience is a way to learn skills that you will need for costume construction. By working on theater productions at the high school or college level, you will begin to learn the techniques that are needed. You may even get some design experience in theater productions.

The Wardrobe Assistant

Being the wardrobe assistant on a movie production is a good way to see what a career in costuming is all about and if you want to work in costuming. You do not have to be able to design costumes or even be skilled in sewing to work as a wardrobe assistant, although on some projects you may be required to have some sewing skills.

The wardrobe assistant helps take care of the costumes during the production. All the costumes are kept on clothing racks that are organized by actor. During production, the assistant hangs them up after the actors have taken them off and keeps them organized. He or she inspects the costumes, once worn, to see if they need any repairs. The assistant also helps launder, iron, and repair the costumes.

The Hairstylist

The style of an actor's hair in a movie production will be determined by the costume designer. The actor's hairstyle must be compatible with the costume and the time in which the movie is set. Hairstylists on movie productions must know how to do hair from different times, like how men and women wore their hair during the Revolutionary War. The hairstyle for the actor may include adding facial hair, like a beard or sideburns. It may include adding a wig or hairpiece. The hair may have to withstand a strong wind or stay in place during a dance number in a scene. Many times the actor will have to dye his or her hair or have it cut in a special way. The hairstylist must be able to do all these things.

Depending on the size of the movie production, there may be several hairstylists as part of the costuming crew. Each star on a production will have his or her own hairstylist. Other hairstylists work on the many other actors and film extras in a production. Sometimes the hairstylist is also trained as a makeup artist. On major motion pictures, hair and makeup are two separate jobs. On smaller productions, they may be performed by one person.

To be a hairstylist on a movie production, you will have to have training in theatrical productions. This includes how to work with wigs and hairpieces. You will also have to know how to construct many different kinds of beards, goatees, and sideburns to fit the actors' faces so that the camera lens will not show that they aren't real. Training for work as a movie hairstylist includes learning how to care for the wigs and hairpieces—how to wash them, store them, and move them from location to location.

Attending a theater arts program and specializing in hair and makeup is one way to get training. You can attend a training program for hairstylists and learn the basic hair styling techniques before getting further training in theatrical hair and makeup techniques. You can also get further training by getting on the crew working with other hairstylists and learning the tricks of the trade.

The Makeup Artist

All actors in a movie production wear makeup. The strong lighting that is used to light the sets, even for outdoor scenes in the daylight, can cause an actor's face to look washed-out or pale. Basic theatrical makeup is applied by the makeup artist to the actors on the set. The makeup artist must be skilled in how to apply theatrical makeup. There are special kinds of makeup and techniques that are used to make the actor's makeup look natural in front of the camera or to achieve special effects.

Makeup is used for many things in a movie besides the obvious purpose of making people look attractive. Makeup is used to make an actor look older or younger. Special effects can be achieved with makeup, like changing a man into a woman. Special items are also constructed. In *Mrs. Doubtfire*, Robin Williams was required to put on a body sack that would turn his masculine build into the plump, rounded figure of an older woman.

Makeup is also used to create effects for an actor who must appear injured. Bruises, scrapes, and bleeding are created with makeup and other techniques. When an actor is shot in a scene, a special bag is placed under the

67

Robin Williams was turned into Mrs. Doubtfire through the use of sophisticated special effects makeup.

actor's clothes. Once the gun is fired, the actor bursts the bag to create the effect of bleeding. The blood is actually made from something as simple as a combination of corn syrup and food coloring.

To be a makeup artist on a movie project, you will have to have special training in how to apply theatrical makeup. You can learn basic makeup techniques in a college or university theater arts program. Film schools may have programs that include course work in makeup. Attending a course or training workshop may also provide some basic training on theatrical makeup techniques. To learn special effects makeup techniques, you will have to take extensive special training.

Once you have special training and some experience in applying makeup, you can get on a makeup crew and learn on the job from makeup artists with years of experience. Like other jobs in the movies, you can work your way up to becoming one of the major makeup artists or a special effects makeup artist.

Sound Production

8

The sound track that you hear while watching a movie, from the opening music, to the voices of the actors, to the honk of horns in traffic, to the explosive noise of gunfire, is created by people who work in sound production. Sound is very important to the movie production. If you didn't have a sound track, you would have a silent picture, like in the days of the first movies before "talkies" were made. But sound production is not one of the glamour professions. People who work in sound production may win awards for sound editing but they don't become famous. Even within the industry, sound is not considered the key part of a production, although it is gaining in importance as movies become more technically sophisticated.

The Sound Editing Process

All the sound for a movie must be recorded, edited, and added to the film. It must be easy to hear and understand and authentic, like the sound you would hear in real life. Some of the sound that is recorded is "natural," that is, recorded during the filming process. The other sound for the movie is "artificial," or added to the film's sound track later, during postproduction.

The sound that is added to a movie is added in two different ways. Live, or natural, sound is recorded on the set as the scene is being filmed. Dialogue that is recorded this way is done with microphones placed on the ends of long poles called booms. The person who is in charge of placing the boom and moving it as needed is the boom operator.

A tape is made of the dialogue during the filming by the production sound mixer. This is the guide track. Later, in the sound recording studio, it provides a guide showing where to replace the dialogue or other sounds. Dialogue is added to the film after shooting in what is called ADR, or automatic dialogue replacement. Dialogue that is added after filming or during the postproduction stage is looped into the sound track. This is an important part of the sound effects editor's job. After filming is finished, the actors are called back to work. The sound effects editor records the dialogue of the actors in the studio and loops this replacement dialogue into the sound track. Sound effects editors also record background voices that you hear in crowd scenes and add these to the sound track.

Most of the sounds that you hear in a movie, from the traffic sounds in an exterior scene to the ticking of a clock in an interior scene, are added later, after the movie has finished filming. These sound effects are added in the controlled environment of the sound recording studio. The sound effects are created on the Foley stage where Foley artists work to reproduce sounds that will seem like the real sounds that you would hear in the natural environment. The Foley stage is a studio that is designed

The sound editor records, adds, and edits all of the dialogue, music, and sound effects of a movie's sound track.

to produce sound effects. Foley artists also provide the sound effects you hear in radio productions.

A third source of sound that is added to the movie sound track is the music. The music is recorded live if it is composed especially for the movie, or it is added from pre-recorded sources. The three sound tracks—the music track, the dialogue track, and the Foley, or sound effects, track—are added to the film in a process called mixing. In the mixing process, the sound mixer works on the three tapes to blend and equalize them into one track of sound. This track is converted to an optical signal so it can be printed along the side of the film. If the sound has been recorded magnetically, it will be bonded to the film.

There are a lot of people working to add sound to a movie production. The jobs in sound recording include the production sound mixer, the boom operator, the third man, the sound effects editor, and the sound mixer. On large films, a sound designer may be hired during the preproduction stage to design the sound that will be used in the movie.

The Production Sound Mixer

The production sound mixer is hired by the production manager or the director during the preproduction stage of making the movie. The production sound mixer's first task is to become familiar with the script and the sound requirements of the movie. He or she will read through the script very carefully and do a script breakdown. A script breakdown is a reading of the script scene by scene to determine the special sound requirements for the movie.

The production sound mixer works with the director on the source of the sound that will be recorded for the movie. Some directors want live sound to come directly from the scene as it is recorded on film. Other directors want the sound to be added later in the studio. The production sound mixer works ahead of actual shooting on the problems of obtaining usable dialogue during the shooting of the movie. During filming, the production sound mixer monitors the sound as it is recorded on a Nagra tape recorder. He or she is in charge of all the sound levels during the shooting of the movie.

The Boom Operator

It is the boom operator's job to position the boom that records the dialogue of the actors. The boom is sometimes called a fish pole because it is a long pole with a microphone attached at its end. The boom is placed over the actors' heads and out of the view of the camera. The boom operator moves the pole from actor to actor as needed, to stay within range for recording the dialogue.

It is also the boom operator's job to keep the microphone out of the shooting frame. The shooting frame is what the camera sees when it shoots the take. The boom operator must know about camera lenses and the viewing angle that each type of lens covers to determine where to place the microphone. He or she cannot run over to the camera viewfinder to see what the frame will look like during filming, and the director is not going to stop shooting to tell the boom operator where to place the microphone.

To learn where to place the boom correctly, the boom operator studies data tables that have information about camera lenses and viewing angles. The boom operator has to memorize this information because there may not be enough time to review the data tables during the shooting of a scene. The boom operator also has to know about lighting. He or she must place the boom so that it does not cast a shadow in the scene that the camera will pick up.

The Third Man

The third man, also called the cable person, places additional microphones that may be needed during a take. These microphones provide an additional source of sound other than what the boom operator picks up. The microphones are hidden in plants or in other out-of-the-way places so that they will not be visible to the camera. The third man also takes care of all the sound cables that are needed for the sound equipment, which is why the job is sometimes called the cable person. When a dolly is being used, the third man watches the sound cable to make sure it stays out of the way of the dolly as it is moving.

Another task of the third man is to check on unwanted noises that may end up being recorded during the take. A car honking or a siren going off in the distance may not be noticed by the director during filming. He or she is too busy focusing on the action of the actors. A door may squeak or an electrical appliance may hum during an interior scene and get picked up by the sound recording equipment. The third man listens through headphones during the rehearsal of a scene to listen for noises that are going to be a problem during the filming.

The Sound Effects Editor

The sound effects editor, sometimes called the supervising sound effects editor if there is a large team of sound editors and assistant sound editors, is in charge of all the sound recording that is made during the production and postproduction stages of the movie. He or she works with the director of the picture to determine what kind of sound will be added and what sources of sound will be used. The sound effects editor is also responsible for the overall quality of the sound production.

During production, the sound effects editor checks the sound tape that is being made by the production sound mixer to see which sound effects are acceptable. The sound effects editor works mostly during the postproduction stage. Once a rough cut of the film is ready, the sound effects editor and the director screen the film to decide where sound needs to be added or replaced. The sound effects editor adds sound to the scene if it has too little sound and will be dead on the screen. Other sounds have to be created, such as the sounds for the visual effects.

The assistant sound editors work with the sound effects editor to create the sound tapes that are added to the movie track. Every sound that is added is on a separate tape. The sound effects editor marks on the final cut of the film where each sound is to be added. Two different sound tracks are created by the sound effects team, one for special effects and one for dialogue. A third track contains the music for the movie.

Once the sound tracks have been completed, the sound effects editor supervises as the sound mixers work during the mixing session. The mixing session is when the three elements of the sound track—the dialogue track, the sound effects track, and the musical score—are mixed. The sound effects editor is forbidden by union rules to do any of the physical mixing of the sound tracks. The director and film editor are also present for the mixing session.

The Foley Artist

The Foley artist's job is to re-create the sounds that you would expect to hear while watching the movie. The Foley artist works with the special effects editor to create the sounds. They work on a Foley stage with many types of equipment made especially for creating different sounds. Foley artists also provide all the sound you hear on radio productions. To work as a Foley artist on a movie, you may have to start in radio production work.

The Sound Mixer

The sound mixer works during the postproduction stage after the movie has been filmed and the sound tracks have been created. The sound tracks are recorded by the sound effects editor and the assistant sound editors. These tracks—the music, dialogue, and special effects—are mixed and equalized by the sound mixer. This means that the volume and intensity of the sounds are mixed to a level appropriate for their location and distance from the camera. The single track of sound that is made is married to the film tape.

The Sound Designer

Like the production manager who oversees all the visual elements of the film, the sound designer designs the sound for the film. He or she coordinates the various aspects of sound production from the live recording that is done on the set to the sound effects that are added after filming. Not all movie productions have a sound designer. But large productions or those that have complex requirements will have a sound designer.

Education and Training

To be a sound designer, you have to have training in sound work. A technical theater degree with emphasis in sound production will provide training in this area. Working or volunteering at a theater or place where you design the sound for various productions will provide you with valuable experience. A technical theater program where you get experience on sound systems for theater productions also provides some training experience.

Sound editors do not make the huge salaries of key people in movie production, like the film editor or art director. The amount you are paid is set by the union, the Motion Picture Editors Guild. If you are working overtime or on call, you will get paid more money. Sound editors who have been working for a while and are in demand for movie projects will make considerably more than union scale.

Film Editing

9

It is the film editor's job to work with and edit the film that is shot during the production stage of the movie. Film editing is the process of selecting the best takes from the ones that have been filmed and putting these scenes into the right sequence, from the beginning of the movie to the end. It takes a film editor and an editing crew to complete this process.

The Film Editing Process

Film editing used to always be completed during the postproduction stage of making a movie, when all the film had been shot and was sent to the editor's workroom. But with the development of computer editing, the film editor can work right along with the film crew, editing the dailies and making the rough cut of the movie for the director as the film is shot.

For most films, however, including smaller independent movies and movies made for businesses, like training films, the film editing process is still mostly done after the shooting has been completed, during the postproduction stage. The editor and director work together, going through the rough cut, refining and making changes to it. Sometimes entire scenes are changed. Rarely, a director will decide a scene does not work and will want to shoot it again, although this is very expensive to do. If the set or location is still available, the crew and actors will have to be brought back to film it.

Today, most film editing is done using a special computer operating system designed specifically for this kind of work. The celluloid film that has been used in the camera is transferred onto the computer and digitized to make it easier to work with. The editor can look at several takes of a scene at one time on the computer screen, then with a click of the mouse select a take and paste it into the scene that is being worked on. If he or she doesn't like it, another click of the mouse cuts it out of the scene. If a mistake is made, it is just a matter of undoing the work and trying something different.

Film used to be edited with a splicing technique. The celluloid film was cut with a razor blade where a scene was to be changed and the new section of film was added, or spliced, into the original section with tape. This was a long and tedious process. With the old film editing process, if a mistake was made, it was very hard to undo and usually wound up on the cutting room floor.

Once the editor has all the scenes edited and put into their proper sequence, the completed rough cut, or "director's cut," is shown to the people involved in the business aspect of the movie production—the producer, the studio executives, and any other financial backers—to get their opinions about the movie. These people may suggest changes to the movie, too. They may say that they don't like a scene, or the music, or they may suggest a different ending to the movie.

The next step in the editing process is to transfer the movie from digital form back to celluloid film. The sound track is then added. It is lined up to match the film negative and married to the film to make a fine cut of the movie. Changes can still be made, however. Test marketing may be done, where the film is shown to test audiences to get their reactions to the movie. Any further changes are made to the film and a final cut is made. It is now ready to be sent to distributors who ship it to the movie theaters.

The Film Editor

A good film editor is as valuable to a movie production as the director of photography or the art director. The film editor has a very important job on a movie project. Depending on the choices the film editor makes in selecting and editing takes of a scene, he or she can totally change the way a movie looks. Because of this, the director hires the film editor that he or she wants to work with. The director wants to make sure that the film editor shares his or her vision of the film and agrees on how the movie should look in its final version. The film editor is hired during the preproduction stage of the film project. He or she is one of the key people on the movie, one of the four department heads who work closely with the director through all stages of the movie production.

It takes experience and a reputation for creative work to get the film editor credit on a movie production. A film editor is hired by a director because he or she is someone the director has worked with before, is known by the director, or is recommended by the producer or someone else in the industry. When considering a film editor for a movie project, the director sends the film editor a movie script to read and then schedules a meeting. At the meeting, the director talks with the film editor about his or her ideas about the script and how the film editor thinks the movie should look once it has been filmed.

To be a film editor, you must think visually. You must be able to think of how the whole picture will look while working with its various parts. It is a job that requires artistic expertise and years of experience. You have to know the details of what makes a good film, from timing to tone, and how the shape and direction of the film can be affected when one scene changes to another.

To become a film editor today, you have to have training in computer editing. You will also have to work your way up, starting in the editing room as an assistant editor, then gaining the experience, trust, and confidence of the editors and directors you work with before you get hired as the film editor, making the editing decisions.

The Assistant Film Editor

All film editors start out as assistant editors. Editing a film is a highly technical skill that takes years of training and experience to perfect. To get started as a film editor, you will have to work on a film as an assistant editor. Assistant editors work with the film editor during the postproduction stage of the movie. The film editor assigns tasks to the assistant as needed.

Education and Training

To work in film editing, you will want to attend a film school or college program that specializes in production work. You will want to get experience in film editing by working on video productions in television. You will have to keep up-to-date on the latest techniques in film editing and the latest developments in equipment. Because of the highly technical aspect of the work today, you will have to have computer training to work in film editing.

Animation and Visual Effects

10

There are more jobs in visual effects today than ever before because of the introduction of computers into moviemaking. From the characters in *Toy Story* to the brilliant special effects in *The Matrix*, computers are changing the look of movies and the possibilities of what you can do when you make a movie. The computer graphics area is growing so rapidly that as recently as 1999 there were not enough people to fill the existing jobs. You could graduate from college with a degree in computer graphics and start a career at a company in the movie industry with a beginning salary of $160,000 a year.

Many areas of the film industry now use computer technology. It is the one skill any film student should have, whether on a business track or for a career in production work like film editing. From shooting the film, to editing it, to adding special effects, to adding sound, computers have made moviemaking faster and more effective. There are many types of jobs in animation and visual effects, including computer animators and model makers.

Animators and Computer Animators

Until very recently, all animated films were made cel by cel. Some animated films continue to be made this way in smaller production companies and for business products. The cel, from "celluloid," is the plastic sheet on which cartoons are drawn. There is one cel, or sheet of plastic, for every film frame of a cartoon. The people who draw the cartoons, animation artists, work mostly on what are called the key frames of the cartoon—the frames where the action or movement of the cartoon figures begin and end. The characters have to be drawn over and over with slight variations to show movement against the background drawings. Because of the number of drawings needed, it takes months of work by a team of animators to get the work done. Lead animators make pencil-and-paper sketches of the characters. The sketches are given to clean-up artists to refine the drawings into clearly drawn characters. Then inkers and painters add the color to produce the final image on the cels. Once completed, the cels are photographed by a special camera and put onto film.

There are many different types of work in an animation studio. To get a job in animation, you must know what kind of work you want to do and specialize in that area of animation. There is the storyboard artist, the layout artist, the model or prop designer, the background painter, and the color key specialist. You can also work in development as someone who creates new ideas.

Before trying to get a job with an animation studio, you must build a portfolio of your artwork. The portfolio should show your best original work; it is better to have a few good samples than several of lesser quality. In the portfolio, include the types of work that might be of interest to the people who are interviewing you. If you want to work as a layout or prop artist, include drawings of places and objects. If you want to work as a character designer, use samples that show expressions and moods. You should make photocopies of the samples to leave with an interviewer, but keep the originals in your portfolio.

With advances in computer graphics, there are more and more careers in computer animation. Computer animation shortens the time needed for the production of the cartoon. This means reduced production costs and less time needed to create a full-length animated film. The computer animator starts with a drawing. The animator draws the character on a key frame at the start of an action sequence and the end of an action sequence. The computer fills in the frames between the two key frames to create the movement of the character. This has revolutionized the amount of time and money needed to make an animated film. It has also changed the number of animators needed to work on the film.

To work as a computer animator, you will have to have training in this area. Attending a two- or four-year college program specializing in computer graphics or attending a film program with special training in computer graphics will be necessary. There are also jobs in the animation industry as production assistants and coordinators. If you want to learn the animation business, this is a good place to begin. You can get an entry-level job with basic office skills and some knowledge of animation.

Industrial Light and Magic, created by the director of *Star Wars*, is the most sophisticated special effects company in Hollywood.

Careers in Visual Effects

The first science-fiction movie, *The Mechanical Butcher*, made in 1895, showed a live pig squeezed into a large box and coming out of the box as bacon, sausage, and spareribs. Did this really happen? Of course not. Trick photography allowed the filmmaker to create this visual effect and make it look like it really happened. Today more and more movies have visual effects as advances are made in the technologies that create those effects. Digital advances in filmmaking, made possible by the invention of the computer, have created a new area of filmmaking and new careers in the movies. Now with the point and click of the computer mouse, computer graphic artists can show producers visual effects faster, cheaper, and more realistically.

Oftentimes, what computers can do in the movies in the way of special effects comes from the way computers are used in other businesses and industries. Spaceships from the movie *Starfighter* were made from the technology developed by the United States Army. Computer use for engineering design and flight simulators was used to develop extraordinary special effects for *Terminator 2* in 1991. The first movie to make extensive use of computer digital effects was *Tron* in 1982, a movie made by Disney.

When you watch a *Star Wars* movie, you see spaceships traveling at light speed and action sequences with fighters battling for control of the planets. The movie *A Bug's Life* showed a microscopic world of critters. These effects were created by people who work in computer graphics and visual effects. The special effects team that started this new momentum in visual effects was assembled by George Lucas, the mastermind behind *Star Wars*. Lucas started Industrial Light and Magic (ILM), the world's leading visual effects company. Lucas and his team were the first ones to use computers in special effects. They developed motion control, a system that fixes cameras to mountings that move in complex, preprogrammed patterns, filming as they move. The ILM lab also helped create the dinosaurs for the movie *Jurassic Park*.

Visual effects careers include work with models and puppets. Movies like the original *King Kong* used a model. The model for King Kong was only eighteen inches tall! Claymation is a stop-motion technique that was used to animate clay figures like Gumby. There are careers as puppet makers and operators. Techniques developed by Jim Henson's Creature Shop, called Animatronics, were used in *Teenage Mutant Ninja Turtles*. There were real actors inside the Ninja turtle suits who controlled the models' movements. The turtles' faces were moved by a puppeteer outside the suits, using cables and radio controls to move the mouths and facial features.

Education and Training

A career in visual effects may begin in different ways. You have to be inventive and very creative. Getting a B.F.A. from a fine arts program or technical production program that includes training in animation and visual effects will provide the background for a career in this area. Computer graphics training will be required for most visual effects careers.

Other Careers

11

There are many other careers in the movies that are part of the process of getting a movie made. The first person to read the movie script when it is sent to the studio by an agent is the story analyst. During the pre-production stage, the casting director helps to find the many actors that are needed for the movie. The composer writes the original music for the movie sound track. It is the location manager's job to find places to shoot the movie scenes that will be filmed on location.

During the production stage, the production manager supervises day-to-day operations and helps to solve any problems that may come up for the different crews that are filming the movie. There may be many vehicles used in a movie production, and it is the transportation captain's job to find all sorts of vehicles, from a Model T Ford to a 2000 Corvette.

Other careers are part of the movie industry but not part of the actual production process. The agent is a very important part of the movie industry. Actors have agents to represent them and help them get auditions for movie roles. Scriptwriters have agents to help them get their movie scripts read and purchased by movie studios. With the money involved in movie projects, entertainment attorneys are becoming more prominent in the movie business. They work on legal issues involved in making a movie and help negotiate the terms of an actor's contract. Other careers include jobs in marketing and public relations and jobs in movie distribution and theater management.

The Story Analyst

The story analyst, more commonly called the reader, is the first person to read a script that is submitted by an agent to the movie studio. For legal reasons, studios usually do not accept submissions that have not been sent in through an agent. Sometimes when a studio has turned down a writer's work and then produced a movie that had some similarity to that writer's script, the writer has sued, claiming the studio used his or her idea for a screenplay.

A typical story analyst reads five to ten scripts a week, or several hundred a year. On average, about one out of ten scripts submitted each week is called to the attention of a studio executive. The reader writes a report on all the scripts and other materials that are reviewed, including novels and magazine articles. The report includes information about the script, a story synopsis, and the reader's recommendations for the script. Sometimes a script is not one the reader likes, but the writer may show talent and the story analyst will note this in the report or recommend the writer to the studio executive for another writing project. Depending on the recommendation of the reader, the executive will scan through the script quickly or read it carefully.

To be a story analyst, you have to be able to recognize good dramatic writing, know which writers are working in the movies, be familiar with what movies have been made, and have a historical perspective on film. You have to understand the structure of a screenplay, where the scenes begin and end, where the dramatic high points of the story are, where the denouement is, and how the characters change and grow. You have to be able to tell what makes a movie work dramatically. It is best to know literary work in general, to have the background to understand scriptwriting and stories that are proposed. You have to be current on what books are out and what other studios may be considering optioning them for movie projects. You also have to know the film business—who is making what movies, what movies are in release, and if they are successful. You have to know the movie market, what kinds of movies people are going to see, and what they want to see in the future.

The Casting Director

The casting director works with the producer to hire additional actors for the movie. The casting director suggests actors, including stars, for roles and assists in the selection process. He or she gets résumés, photographs, and video examples of actors' work to show to the producer and director. The casting director holds auditions to fill some of the roles, including roles for extras. Additional duties may include helping with the contract negotiations between an actor's agent or attorney and the producer.

To work as a casting agent, you have to know the movie business and movie scripts. You have to know stories and characters. You have to have a sense of what a character will be like on screen and what kind of actor will make that character believable. A background in theater arts, human resources, or public relations will help you prepare for a career as a casting director.

The Composer

The composer of the musical score is an important part of the movie production. The sound track enhances the visual effects of the movie and creates a mood for the audience. Sometimes the movie sound track is what brings people in to see a movie. The director works with the composer to determine what kind of music the movie will have and when music should be played during the movie. The composer starts working on original music for the sound track during the preproduction stage of the movie. After the movie is filmed, the composer screens the movie to make cues, guides or markers indicating where music will be added, and to time the scene to determine how long the music should be. Once the score is completed, musicians are hired to record the music and it is recorded on a sound track. The track is added to the film by the sound mixer.

The Production Manager

The production manager is hired by the producer to supervise the day-to-day aspects of the movie project. The production manager is on the set every day to oversee the film crews and to make sure that the production is going smoothly. The production manager reports to the producer, keeping him or her informed of daily operations. Together they troubleshoot, or solve problems that come up during the production process. The production manager also helps to set up location shootings and makes sure film extras are available for certain scenes.

To be a production manager, you must have excellent organizational skills, work well at many tasks at one time, be able to supervise other people, have a thorough understanding of film production, and have a strong business background. A background in business management, film production, or technical theater will be helpful. Working on a movie project in different jobs will help you learn production work. To be a production manager, you have to know the moviemaking business from end to end.

The Location Manager

The location manager works during the preproduction stage to scout locations for filming. The location manager travels to areas that are being considered to determine if the sites are appropriate for the scene and what production requirements will be needed. The location manager looks for locations that meet requirements established by the director and the director of photography.

Script Continuity

Sometimes it takes more than one take, or even more than one day, to film a scene. If someone walks off with a particular prop and doesn't bring it back for the next day's shoot, the movie might contain disturbing

A location manager finds the right country for filming; for example, the movie *Braveheart* was filmed in Ireland and Scotland.

inconsistencies. The audience might see an actor walk by a table with a vase on it, and then walk back past a vaseless table a minute later. The person who works on script continuity stands by the camera operator during filming and records all the details of a scene as it is being filmed. This information is put on a continuity report. The information includes exactly where the actor moves, where her hand is, in what hand she is holding a soft drink, what food is served if she is eating a meal, and what dialogue may have been changed during the filming. This helps to keep track of what was in a scene so that other takes have the same setup.

The Clapper Loader

Before each take, a slate is placed in front of the camera on which the number of the take is written. At the top of the slate is an arm that lifts and closes with a clapping noise. At the start of the take, it is the clapper loader's job to call out the name of the movie and the number of the take, and then clap down the arm on the slate board. This provides a visual and auditory cue to the editor when he or she is working with the takes during the film editing process. After the take, the clapper loader records the shot on the picture negative report sheet along with information about the take, like the camera magazine number, length of film stock, the length of the take, whether it is an interior or exterior shot, or a day or night shot. Takes that are not to be printed are marked outtakes, usually the result of a mistake that was made during the shooting. The picture negative report sheet accompanies the can of film to the laboratory.

The Entertainment Attorney

The entertainment attorney specializes in drafting and evaluating contracts and agreements that must be worked out before a movie project can get under way. Sometimes entertainment attorneys also work as agents, representing their clients and helping to get them movie roles. Because of the large salaries and benefits that may be included in an actor's contract, entertainment attorneys are oftentimes involved in the negotiating of contracts with the movie studio. The terms of an actor's contract may determine if the actor gets a percentage of the box office receipts or whether or not the actor will participate in stunt work. To be an entertainment attorney, you have to have a law degree specializing in contracts and experience in the entertainment business.

The Agent

To work as an actor or writer in the movies, you have to have an agent or belong to a union. It is the agent's job to get an actor work. Hollywood agents are well-connected, meaning they know the right people to talk to. Producers, casting agents, and directors work directly with agents when casting actors for movie roles. An agent will arrange for an actor to get an audition for a movie role and then contact the actor about the audition. Once an actor is offered a movie role, the agent helps to negotiate the contract for the actor. An agent usually works for a talent agency and will have many actors as clients.

Writers in Hollywood have agents to help them get their scripts read and optioned for movie production. Agents contact the studios and get the movie scripts read by story analysts. A college degree in marketing and public relations, mass communications, or a related area will help you prepare for a career as an agent. It is a bonus to have a law degree. Some entertainment attorneys work as agents for their clients as well as representing them in legal matters.

There are many other jobs in the film industry that have nothing to do with the actual production of the movie. There are careers in marketing and publicity. There are careers for people who work on making the trailers—the preview of the movie you see at the theater and on television commercials. There are careers in rating the movie for the movie rating system, and careers for people whose job it is to sell a movie to theater distributors in other countries.

Getting Started in a Film Career

12

Once you have graduated from a college or training program, you will have to live where movies are being made. If you want to work regularly in the feature film industry, you will probably have to move to Los Angeles; New York; Chicago; Wilmington, North Carolina; or Orlando, Florida—the cities with the most movie productions in the United States—with Los Angeles and New York at the top of the list. Increasingly, movies are being filmed on location, in smaller cities and in the Midwest where production costs are lower, so it is possible to get some film production work in these areas.

Getting Your First Job

Probably more than any other business, getting into moviemaking is a matter of contacts. Most jobs in Hollywood go to someone who knows someone. Jimmy got a job as a runner on a movie production because Jimmy's uncle works as a gaffer and told the production manager that he was a good person for the job. Even though Jimmy hopes to work as a lighting technician and has a two-year degree from a technical school in electrical systems and lighting, he was excited to get this first job on a movie production. When Jimmy reports to the set each day, he will watch the lighting technicians work and talk to the crew members during their breaks when he is not running errands for the production manager. On a future movie project, Jimmy hopes one of the crew will recommend him for a job on the lighting crew.

If you have a contact, even if it is someone who works in an area of movie production that you do not plan to work in, you may be able to get your foot in the door. Calling that person may lead to another contact in the area you do want to work in. You can start your list of contacts by getting names from your college or training program staff. Many times alumni are working in the career area you want to go into. Asking teachers and professors if they know someone who is working in film production is a good way to get contacts. You may also be able to get contacts from other sources. A former neighbor or someone in your hometown may know of someone working in the business. If you tell people you are trying to get started in film production work, they may suggest someone you can call. You can also contact people who are working in your area on some aspect of film or video work. Someone working on independent film projects or video production work may have suggestions for contacts or a way to get a first job.

You can also get that first job by contacting people who are working in the business and asking to talk to them about their work. You can get a list of people from the union or guild for that career, then start making phone calls. Become familiar with a person's work so you can talk about it and about your interest in his or her work. Knocking on doors with your résumé and credentials in hand is a hard way to look for work, but it may get you an interview or a job offer.

To get a first job you have to be prepared to start at the entry level, as a runner or an assistant, whatever it takes to get on a movie set. Once there, through observation and talking to people about their jobs, you can learn more about movie production work and opportunities for your next job.

What's Ahead in the Movie Job Market?

If you are going to work in the film industry today, you will need computer training of some kind. Even if your job does not directly use computers, you will benefit from computer training because you will understand the editing process and know about computer animation. The growth area of jobs in the movie industry is in computer graphics.

If you want a job in the film industry, you should keep up with new developments and technologies by reading periodicals about the industry. Most of them are listed in *Ulrich's International Periodicals Directory*, which should be available at your public library. The heading "motion pictures" will list many of them. Others will be listed under "communications—radio and television."

Unions and Guilds

To work in the film industry, you have to understand the role that unions play. Most jobs in the film industry are

In your first job, be prepared to start at the entry level.

union jobs. Where movie production is unionized, people work on clearly defined tasks. For example, if it is a union shoot, a scrim must be set up by a grip. But if the scrim needs to be placed on the lamp itself, it must be put in place by an electrician.

The union sets the minimum scale, or the base pay for its members. It negotiates working conditions, such as how many hours you can work each day. The Screen Actors Guild, or SAG, is the union that represents actors. It works to guarantee standard working conditions, wages, pensions, and health benefits for the actors who are members. To find out what union controls a particular area of film production, refer to the reference material at the back of this book. This will also give you an indication of what the current wage scale is for a particular skill.

Film Schools

Not surprisingly, film schools started on the West Coast, where the movies began. There are film programs of some kind in most areas of the country, though. Whether it be a summer training program or a full-length four-year degree program, there are likely to be training opportunities in your area. Some film programs have been around a long time and are known for their famous graduates and the quality of their programs. These are competitive programs that accept a limited number of new students each year. To find a film training program in your area, contact the state board of higher education or the state film commission office, or contact one of the film schools listed at the back of this book.

Film Schools

Art Center College of Design

Pasadena, California

The Art Center College of Design offers a film/video program staffed by practicing artists and designers. Students study cinematography, lighting, production design, directing, editing, and writing. The undergraduate and graduate programs explore all aspects of the film industry from feature film to documentary to commercials to industrial videos. For more information write to Film Department, Art Center College of Design, 1700 Lida Street, Pasadena, CA 91103-1999, (818) 584-5000. Web site: http://www.artcenter.edu.

California Institute of the Arts (CalArts)

Valencia, California

CalArts was the first degree-granting institution of higher learning created specifically for students of the visual and performing arts. The School of Film/Video provides work in dramatic, documentary, and experimental film/video, studio and video production, and character and computer animation. Students have access to CMX computer video editing and the motion control camera. Study is in four areas of concentration: live action, experimental animation, character animation (undergraduate), and directing for theater and cinema. For more information contact Film/Video Counselor, California Institute of the Arts, 24700 McBean Parkway, Valencia, CA 91355, (661) 255-1050, (800) 292-ARTS (California), (800) 545-ARTS (other states). Web site: http://www.calarts.edu.

Columbia College

Chicago, Illinois

Course training emphasizes practical experience in the craft of filmmaking. Concentrations are offered in production, management, screenwriting, and critical studies. Graduating filmmakers make an individual film, which serves as a résumé for future job hunting. Columbia College's graduate division offers an M.F.A. in film/video. For more information contact the Admissions Office, Columbia College, 600 South Michigan Avenue, Chicago, IL 60605, (312) 663-1600. Web site: http://www.colum.edu.

Indiana University

Bloomington, Indiana

Offers film studies as an interdepartmental program that uses humanities to examine film as a cultural project. Undergraduate students major in comparative literature or telecommunications while taking film courses to obtain film studies certificates. The program also offers a doctoral minor in film studies. For more information contact Director, Film Studies, Ballantine Hall 306, Indiana University, Bloomington, IN 47405-6613, (812) 855-1072. Web site: http://www.indiana.edu

New York Film Academy

New York, New York

A relatively new program that offers basic and advanced courses in hands-on film production. Courses are short, lasting eight to ten weeks. B.F.A. degrees are available through affiliated schools. For more information contact Director, New York Film Academy, 100 East 17th Street, New York, NY 10003, (212) 674-4300. Web site: http://www.nyfa.com.

New York University
Tisch School of the Arts

New York, New York

Offers undergraduate and graduate training in film, video, television, radio, cinema studies, and dramatic writing. The undergraduate program combines professional training with a basic liberal arts education. Graduate degrees include an M.F.A. in film or dramatic writing or an M.A. or Ph.D. in cinema studies. For more information contact Portfolio Coordinator, Tisch School of the Arts, 721 Broadway, New York, NY 10003-6807, (212) 998-1820. Web site: http://www.nyu.edu/tisch.

University of California (UCLA)

Los Angeles, California
This program offers film courses through the School of Theater, Film, and Television. Undergraduate students study criticism, screenwriting, production, and animation. Study abroad and internship programs are offered. An M.F.A. in film/television production, screenwriting, or animation is offered. An M.F.A. or Ph.D. in critical studies is also offered. For more information contact UCLA School of Theater, Film, and Television, at 102 East Melnitz Hall, Box 951622, Los Angeles, CA 90095-1622, (310) 825-5761. Web site: http://www.ucla.edu.

University of Central Florida School of Film

Orlando, Florida
Four-year programs leading to a B.A. in either motion picture technology or radio/television. Film students specialize in either screenwriting and production or in animation. For more information contact the Motion Picture Division at P.O. Box 160000, Orlando, FL 32816, (407) 823-2000. Web site: http://www.ucf.edu

University of Southern California

Los Angeles, California
The first film school in the nation, it offers both undergraduate and graduate degrees with a liberal arts education. The Critical Studies Program offers studies in two

areas: film history, including world and Hollywood cinema, and the history of film theory, or television and video history. Studies also include film production and the basics of writing short and feature-length screenplays. Includes an internship program. The Production Program is a two-year program that includes instruction in camera, sound, editing, screenwriting, directing of actors, and directing of cameras. Students have the opportunity to produce a major production their senior year. The Film Writing Program is a four-year B.F.A. program that provides undergraduates with practice in screenwriting with an emphasis on combining film form and film content. The Graduate Screenwriting Program is a two-year course of instruction concentrating on writing for narrative film and television and grants a M.F.A. degree. The Peter Stark Motion Picture Producing Program is a full-time graduate program that concentrates on the business of filmmaking, including production, licensing, marketing, and distribution issues. For more information contact School of Cinema-Television, University of Southern California, University Park, Los Angeles, CA 90089, (213) 740-2311. Web site: http://www.usc.edu.

Film Careers

By Job Title

actor The actors play the principal and supporting roles in a movie. In big-budget pictures the principal actors are stars, or famous actors, who will draw people in to see the movie.

agent The talent agent represents actors and assists them in getting movie roles, including arranging for auditions and helping actors negotiate the terms of their contracts.

animator/computer animator The animator works for an animation studio drawing cartoons or some aspect of the animated feature. Computer animators are graphic artists who draw and design cartoon figures using the computer.

art director/production designer The art director or production designer designs the sets for the movie and is responsible for the look of the sets and locations.

best boy The best boy is the head electrican's main assistant.

boom operator The boom operator maneuvers the sound boom during filming to record the dialogue of the actors.

camera assistant The camera assistant is a member of the camera crew who assists the camera operator as the focus puller and by loading film into the camera.

camera operator The camera operator runs the camera to film the scenes for the movie.

carpenter/prop maker The movie carpenter or prop maker builds the sets for the movie.

casting director The casting director recommends actors to play the leading parts in a movie and casts people for additional roles.

clapper loader The clapper loader is in charge of the clapper, which is used to signal the start of each take of a movie scene.

composer The composer writes the original music score for the movie.

costume designer The costume designer designs the costumes for the movie and may help construct or purchase the costumes for the actors.

costumer The costumer constructs costumes for the actors and has them fitted.

Careers in the Movies

director The director is in charge of the filming of the movie. He or she is the creative force behind the movie, interpreting the screenplay.

director of photography The director of photography, also called the cinematographer, photographs the film and is in charge of the quality of photography and lighting on the movie.

entertainment attorney The entertainment attorney assists with litigation, negotiating contracts, and other legal matters for a film studio.

film editor The film editor edits the footage of film that has been shot and works with the director to create a final cut of the movie that is distributed to the movie theaters.

film extra Film extras are actors and nonactors who have nonspeaking roles in the cast.

Foley artist The Foley artist creates sound effects on a Foley stage.

gaffer The gaffer is the head electrician on a film unit in charge of lighting the set. He or she works with the director of photography on how to light the scenes, hires the lighting crew, and supervises the setting up of the lights for each scene.

grip The grip is a nontechnical member of the lighting crew. He or she moves props from scene to scene, builds platforms and other structures, lays track for the camera on location, and puts camera and sound recording equipment in place.

hairstylist The hairstylist styles the hair of the actors and prepares wigs and hairpieces as needed for the costuming of the movie.

key grip The key grip makes sure that the cameras are set up, moves the cameras to other locations, and operates the crane for the camera operator.

lighting technician The lighting technician places and focuses the lights for a movie scene.

location manager The location manager scouts locations needed for shooting.

makeup artist The makeup artist applies makeup to the actors. Special effects makeup artists provide any special makeup effects needed.

nursery man The nursery man provides foliage needed to assist with the lighting requirements on the set.

producer The producer is responsible for the overall movie production. He or she hires the director and assists the director in hiring the other key people on the movie project. The producer is responsible for keeping the movie under budget. The producer may also get financial backing for the movie.

production manager The production manager makes a schedule for filming the scenes of the movie. He or she is in charge of the crew and makes sure everything is moved from one location to the next.

production sound mixer The production sound mixer runs the sound equipment to record the sound on the movie set.

property master The property master supplies the props for the sets for a movie scene and makes sure they are in place before filming.

script supervisor (continuity) The script supervisor, or the person in charge of script continuity, makes detailed notes of the scene as it is filmed. These notes are made into a continuity report and are used to make sure that the scene looks the same for the next take.

scriptwriter The scriptwriter writes the original screenplay that is made into a movie, or is hired by a studio to rewrite a screenplay for a movie production.

set decorator The set decorator decorates the set after it has been painted.

set designer The set designer draws the blueprints and plans for the sets.

sound designer The sound designer designs the sound for a movie project.

sound effects editor The sound effects editor is in charge of the overall quality of sound and sound levels on a movie production.

sound mixer The sound mixer combines, or mixes, and equalizes the special effects track, dialogue track, and music track into one track.

special effects model maker The model maker makes the models for special and visual effects.

standby painter The standby painter is part of the photography crew and paints surfaces that may need to be modified for lighting purposes.

stills photographer The stills photographer takes pictures during the production of the movie for a record of the production and to use for publicity purposes.

story analyst The story analyst, or reader, reads movie scripts that have been submitted to a studio by an agent.

stunt artist The stunt artist performs the stunts for the movie. The stunt double stands in for the star actor when required.

stunt coordinator The stunt coordinator organizes the work of the stunt artists and is in charge of setting up the stunts during filming.

third man The third man is on the sound crew and places microphones that are needed in a scene.

transportation captain The transportation captain is responsible for getting the vehicles needed for the movie production and taking care of them during the production.

wardrobe assistant The wardrobe assistant assists the actors with their costumes during the filming of the movie.

By Department

KEY PEOPLE
Producer
Director
Scriptwriter

ACTORS/STUNT ARTISTS
Actor
Film Extra
Stunt Coordinator
Stunt Artist

PHOTOGRAPHY
Director of Photography
Best Boy
Camera Operator
Camera Assistant
Stills Photographer

LIGHTING
Gaffer
Lighting Technician
Key Grip
Grip
Standby Painter
Nursery Man

SET DESIGN
Art Director/
    Production Designer
Set Designer
Set Decorator
Carpenter/Props Maker
Property Master

COSTUMING/MAKEUP
Costume Designer
Costumer
Wardrobe Assistant
Hairstylist
Makeup Artist

SOUND PRODUCTION
Sound Designer
Production Sound Mixer
Boom Operator
Third Man
Sound Effects Editor
Foley Artists
Sound Mixer

FILM EDITING
Film Editor
Film Editor's Assistant

ANIMATION AND VISUAL EFFECTS
Animator and Computer
    Animator
Visual Effects Artist
Model Maker

OTHER CAREERS
Story Analyst
Casting Director
Composer
Production Manager
Location Manager
Script Supervisor
Clapper Loader
Transportation Captain
Entertainment Attorney
Agent

Glossary

ADR Automatic dialogue replacement that is added to a sound track after filming.

cel The plastic sheet on which cartoons are drawn.

clapper board A slate board on which the number of a take is written. The board is placed in front of the camera at the start of filming to track the take for editing purposes.

claymation A stop-motion technique used to animate clay figures.

continuity report A complete record of a day's work at the end of a day of filming.

crane A long, pivoted boom mounted on a wheeled trolley. It has a platform at the end of the boom where the director, camera operator, and an assistant can sit to watch and film the action.

credits The list of creative contributors at the end of the movie.

cutting room The editor's workroom.

dailies Each day's takes of scenes that were filmed. The directors and producers view the dailies the evening after filming or the next morning to see how the scenes look and what needs to be refilmed.

dialogue looping Adding dialogue to the sound track after the sound has been recorded.

digital effects Special effects made on the computer.

dolly A wheeled platform on which a camera is mounted so it can move for traveling shots.

exterior scene A scene that is filmed outside.

fine cut The cut of a movie that is worked on before it is released for distribution to the movie theaters.

fishpole The pole or boom that holds a microphone above the actors during filming.

floor The set of the soundstage.

head shot An 8 1/2-by-11 black-and-white photograph of an actor used to show to casting directors and agents as part of the actor's résumé.

interior scene A movie scene that is filmed inside.

lamps Lights used to light the scenes in a movie shoot.

married To put together on film. The sound track is married to the film.

music score Music written for a movie by a composer or musician.

premier The first public screening of a new movie. The main purpose is for publicity, with lots of celebrities and stars from the movie in attendance.

properties/props The moveable items used to decorate and furnish a set to make it look lived in. Some props are specially made for a film, some are supplied by the studio props departments, and others are purchased for the film.

release print The thousands of copies of the movie that are made and distributed to movie theaters.

rigging The process of setting up the lighting for a movie scene.

rough cut The takes of a movie that are assembled as the movie is being filmed, also called the director's cut. It is a working version of the film to allow changes before a final cut of the film is made.

scoring studio A soundstage equipped with a screen, where the orchestra works to record the music track for the film.

script breakdown Breaking a screenplay into scenes and takes for shooting purposes.

silent picture A movie with no sound added.

soundstage A soundproof studio with a complete lighting rig for filming interior scenes of a movie.

sound track The dialogue, special effects, and music that are added to the film.

splice To cut and tape two sections of celluloid film together.

take A filmed section of a movie scene.

talkies The first movies that had sound and dialogue added.

union/guild A professional organization that helps its members negotiate working conditions, including basic salary requirements and work schedules.

visual effects The special effects that are added to a movie.

For More Information

Industry Periodicals

American Cinematographer
Box 2230
Hollywood, CA 90078

American Film
The American Film Institute
3 East 54th Street
New York, NY 10022

Back Stage
1515 Broadway, 14th Floor
New York, NY 10036

Boxoffice
Suite 100
6640 Sunset Boulevard
Hollywood, CA 90028

Daily Variety
5700 Wilshire Boulevard, Suite 120
Hollywood, CA 90036

Hollywood Reporter
5055 Wilshire Boulevard
Los Angeles, CA 90036-4396

Independent Film and Video Monthly
625 Broadway, 9th Floor
New York, NY 10012

Millimeter
5 Penn Plaza, 13th Floor
New York, NY 10001

Variety
245 West 17th Street
New York, NY 10011

Videography
460 Park Avenue, 9th Floor
New York, NY 10016

Video Week
2115 Ward Court NW
Washington, DC 20037

Web Sites

American Cinema Editors (ACE)
http://www.ace-filmeditors.org

American Society of Cinematographers
http://www.cinematographer.com

Cyber Film School
http://www.cyberfilmschool.com

Directors Guild of America
http://www.dga.org

International Animated Film Society
http://asifa-hollywood.org

Internet Movie Database
http://imdb.com

Motion Picture Editors Guild
http://www.editorsguild.com

Motion Picture Sound Editors
http://www.mpse.org

Rhythm and Hues Studios
http://www.rhythm.com

Society of Motion Pictures and Television Engineers
http://www.smpte.org

Variety On-Line
http://www.variety.com

Visual Effects Headquarters
http://www.vfxhq.com

Visual Effects Resource Center
http://www.visualfx.com/library.htm

Women in Film
http://www.wif.org

Writers Guild of America
http://www.wga.org

For Further Reading

Bone, Jan. *Opportunities in Film Careers.* Lincoln-wood, IL: VGM Career Horizons, 1998.

Coulter, George, and Shirley Coulter. *Movies: You Make It Work.* Vero Beach, FL: Rourke Publications, Inc., 1996.

Cross, Robin. *Movie Magic: A Behind-the-Scenes Look at Filmmaking.* New York: Sterling Publishing, 1995.

Everson, William K. *The American Movie.* New York: Atheneum, 1963.

Goldreich, Gloria, and Esther Goldreich. *What Can She Be? A Film Producer.* New York: Lothrop, Lee & Shepard Co., 1977.

Manchel, Frank. *Movies and How They Are Made.* Engelwood Cliffs, NJ: Prentice-Hall, 1968.

Manchel, Frank. *When Pictures Began to Move.* Engelwood Cliffs, NJ: Prentice-Hall, 1969.

Morgan, Bradley J., and Joseph M. Palmisano, eds.. *Film and Video Career Directory.* Washington, DC: Gale Research Inc., 1994.

Taub, Eric. *Gaffers, Grips, and Best Boys.* New York: St. Martin's Press, 1994.

Index

Photo Credits

Cover © Corbis; pp. 4, 39, 45 © AP/Worldwide; pp. 9, 15, 27, 63, 68, 85A, 85B © Everett Collection; p. 32 © *The Tennessean*/AP/Worldwide; pp. 55, 99 © FPG International; p. 71 © Corbis; p. 97 © Andrew Cooper/Everett Collection.

Design

Danielle Goldblatt

Layout

Geri Giordano